Transition to a Free Market

Studies in the Regulation of Economic Activity
TITLES PUBLISHED

The Dilemma of Freight Transport Regulation
Ann F. Friedlaender

Technological Change in Regulated Industries
William M. Capron, Editor

Reforming Regulation: An Evaluation of the Ash Council Proposals
A staff paper by Roger G. Noll

International Diffusion of Technology: The Case of Semiconductors
John E. Tilton

Public Policy toward General Aviation
Jeremy J. Warford

The Local Service Airline Experiment
George C. Eads

Economic Aspects of Television Regulation
Roger G. Noll, Merton J. Peck, and John J. McGowan

Government and the Sports Business
Roger G. Noll, Editor

Energy Regulation by the Federal Power Commission
Stephen G. Breyer and Paul W. MacAvoy

Economic Regulation of Domestic Air Transport: Theory and Policy
George W. Douglas and James C. Miller III (out of print)

Social Responsibility and the Business Predicament
James W. McKie, Editor

Bread upon the Waters: Federal Aids to the Maritime Industries
Gerald R. Jantscher

Promoting Competition in Regulated Markets
Almarin Phillips, Editor

Transition to a Free Market: Deregulation of the Air Cargo Industry
A staff paper by Andrew S. Carron

Studies in the Regulation of Economic Activity

Transition to a Free Market: Deregulation of the Air Cargo Industry

A Staff Paper by Andrew S. Carron

THE BROOKINGS INSTITUTION
Washington, D.C.

1775 Massachusetts Avenue, N.W., Washington, D.C. 20036

Library of Congress Cataloging in Publication data:

Carron, Andrew S.
Transition to a free market.
(Studies in the regulation of economic activity)
Includes bibliographical references.
1. Aeronautics, Commercial—United States—Freight. 2. Aeronautics, Commercial—Freight—Law and legislation—United States. 3. Trade regulation—Economic aspects—United States. I. Title. II. Series.
HE9788.5.U5C37 387.7'44'0973 81-10244
ISBN 0-8157-1297-9 (pbk.) AACR2

1 2 3 4 5 6 7 8 9

THE BROOKINGS INSTITUTION is an independent organization devoted to nonpartisan research, education, and publication in economics, government, foreign policy, and the social sciences generally. Its principal purposes are to aid in the development of sound public policies and to promote public understanding of issues of national importance.

The Institution was founded on December 8, 1927, to merge the activities of the Institute for Government Research, founded in 1916, the Institute of Economics, founded in 1922, and the Robert Brookings Graduate School of Economics and Government, founded in 1924.

The Board of Trustees is responsible for the general administration of the Institution, while the immediate direction of the policies, program, and staff is vested in the President, assisted by an advisory committee of the officers and staff. The by-laws of the Institution state: "It is the function of the Trustees to make possible the conduct of scientific research, and publication, under the most favorable conditions, and to safeguard the independence of the research staff in the pursuit of their studies and in the publication of the results of such studies. It is not a part of their function to determine, control, or influence the conduct of particular investigations or the conclusions reached."

The President bears final responsibility for the decision to publish a manuscript as a Brookings book. In reaching his judgment on the competence, accuracy, and objectivity of each study, the President is advised by the director of the appropriate research program and weighs the views of a panel of expert outside readers who report to him in confidence on the quality of the work. Publication of a work signifies that it is deemed a competent treatment worthy of public consideration but does not imply endorsement of conclusions or recommendations.

The Institution maintains its position of neutrality on issues of public policy in order to safeguard the intellectual freedom of the staff. Hence interpretations or conclusions in Brookings publications should be understood to be solely those of the authors and should not be attributed to the Institution, to its trustees, officers, or other staff members, or to the organizations that support its research.

Foreword

The case for regulatory reform is often made by comparing the current performance of an industry with its expected performance under a new regulatory regime. But discussion on how to improve ultimate efficiency too often glosses over the gains and losses that would be occasioned by the transition. Those gains and losses are likely to involve property rights, the ability of producers and consumers to adapt, and the ability of the market to function while undergoing changes.

The deregulation movement is well under way, but few industries have yet been completely deregulated. Though they are being phased out, some rate and entry controls still apply to the passenger airline, natural gas, trucking, railroad, consumer banking, private-line telecommunications, and telephone toll service industries. Of the few from which all economic controls have been removed, the air cargo industry provides particularly valuable information, much of it of general usefulness. And because the industry has been deregulated for more than two years, the important directions of change can be detected even though adjustment to the new free-market environment is not yet complete.

The need to understand the transition costs of deregulation was recognized by a panel of experts convened in February 1978 by the National Science Foundation to discuss future directions for research on government regulation. That conference, and subsequent discussions with some of the participants, motivated the author of this staff paper to analyze the process of adaptation in the context of a case study, so as to devise rules that would make deregulation of other industries less costly and more easily administered.

Andrew S. Carron is a research associate in the Brookings Economic Studies program. He is indebted to his Brookings colleagues Robert W.

Crandall and Theodore E. Keeler for helpful comments on drafts of this paper, to Paul W. MacAvoy and Merton J. Peck of Yale University for their assistance in his research and to George W. Douglas for numerous helpful suggestions. Richard B. Thomas and Timothy A. Cohn provided computer assistance. The manuscript was edited by Diane Hammond and checked for accuracy by Penelope Harpold.

This paper is based on a doctoral dissertation at Yale University that was supported in part by a Brookings research fellowship. It is the fourteenth publication in the Brookings series of Studies in the Regulation of Economic Activity. The series is devoted to presenting the results of research focused on public policies toward business and is supported by grants from the Ford Foundation, the Alfred P. Sloan Foundation, and the Alex C. Walker Foundation.

The views expressed here are those of the author and should not be ascribed to the organizations whose assistance is acknowledged above or to the trustees, officers, or other staff members of the Brookings Institution.

BRUCE K. MAC LAURY
President

July 1981
Washington, D.C.

Transition to a Free Market: Deregulation of the Air Cargo Industry

Until the late 1970s, the transportation and public utility industries operated under government regulations dating from the previous century. Regulation of prices and entry had generated misallocations and inefficiencies in production, profits were down, and the quality of service appeared to have deteriorated. A consensus was reached by legislators, industry groups, academics, and consumer representatives on a new regulatory environment. Within a few years virtually every one of these industries was deregulated.

The last issue to be resolved was the transition from the old regime of tight controls to the new regime of looser controls. Elaborate phasing schemes were built. However, the theoretical base was thin and deregulation was new and untried, although the process by which firms, consumers, and regulators adjust to the new rules can have important economic implications during transition and may affect the likelihood of attaining the desired end.

One of the few industries from which all economic controls have been removed, and therefore one which can be instructive for others, is the air cargo industry. What is more, regulation has been completely lifted from this industry since 1978, so directions of change can be detected even though its adjustment to the free market is not complete.

Background

The modern air cargo industry got its start during the closing years of World War II as new aircraft, until then preempted by the military, became available to the commercial airlines. Between 1944 and 1947 there was widespread entry, largely through the acquisition of inexpensive surplus aircraft by operators exempt from regulation.

Literally hundreds of small all-cargo airlines were created, most seeking to serve previously untapped markets with unknown revenue potential. There was clearly too much capacity for the demand, and most carriers incurred large operating losses. Many went bankrupt. Safety standards deteriorated.

At first the Civil Aeronautics Board permitted these new carriers rate and route freedom, as it had no basis on which to judge applications for cargo certificates. (In many ways, CAB policy toward all-cargo carriers was as liberal as that under the deregulation amendments.) In 1947, the CAB began regulating the route and rate flexibility of all airlines transporting cargo, paralleling the controls applied to passenger service. Several all-cargo carriers were certificated, but between 1947 and 1956 there was nearly as much exit (via bankruptcy or merger) as entry. After 1956, no new all-cargo airlines were certificated. By 1977 only three all-cargo carriers were still in operation. Early failures and lack of new entry were more the result of excess supply and low profit expectations than of the CAB's entry controls.[1]

Domestic rates were deregulated in November 1977. Entry controls on domestic scheduled cargo service for firms already engaged in scheduled air transportation were removed January 9, 1978 (a few months later for charter airlines). Beginning in May 1979 new carriers could enter the industry subject only to tests of fitness, willingness, and ability to serve.

Demand and Supply

There are two principal reasons for a shipper to select the air mode over surface transportation. One, the speed of air transportation, especially over long distances, is an advantage for goods subject to spoilage and those requiring next-morning delivery in the domestic market. Two, air transportation's low risk of losing or damaging shipments is an advantage for goods

1. Passenger airlines were permitted to carry cargo in any type of aircraft over any route for which they had passenger authority. In the early 1970s, the unregulated commuter air carrier sector began transporting significant amounts of cargo, but exclusively in small aircraft. Operators of small aircraft (originally defined by the Civil Aeronautics Board as having 7,500 pounds of payload capacity or less, also referred to as air taxis) could offer scheduled or nonscheduled passenger or cargo service without being subject to CAB economic regulation under the "commuter air carrier" exemption.

with a high ratio of value to size. Shipping charges for these valuable and time-sensitive goods are usually small in comparison with the value of the items. However, because there are often few reasonable alternatives to air shipment, demand for this prime-time service is relatively insensitive to its price. To increase utilization of aircraft and facilities at other times, carriers offer lower rates for shipping specific commodities that do not need to move at prime time and would not move by air at standard rates. Thus, unless corrected for quality of service, demand for air cargo services will appear more price elastic than it is.

Shippers may tender their freight directly to the airline or use the services of an air freight forwarder. The forwarders provide pickup and delivery services, consolidate small packages into large shipments, and contract with direct air carriers for the line-haul (airborne) portion of the trip.

Supplying air cargo transportation requires a number of specialized inputs, but aircraft represent the single largest and longest-lived of the capital inputs, the factor most susceptible to technological change, and the one to which most other inputs are complementary. The choice and use of flight and ground personnel, fuel, freight handling equipment, and maintenance facilities are almost completely determined by the choice and use of aircraft.

Cargo may be carried in the belly compartment of a passenger (combination) aircraft or in a freighter aircraft configured exclusively for that use.[2] In most combination aircraft, the relative quantities of main-deck passenger capacity and below-deck cargo capacity (belly) are fixed by the design requirement that aircraft have a circular cross section.[3] Thus passenger and cargo capacity may be considered the joint products of a combi-

2. Virtually all airlines transport cargo; some passenger airlines use both combination aircraft and freighters. Some airlines handle cargo strictly on a charter basis, while most scheduled airlines also perform some charter work.

3. The assumption of fixed proportions is not meant to imply that all aircraft types (or even all aircraft of a given type) have the same ratio of cargo to passenger capacity. Combination aircraft may be configured with the galley on the main deck to increase below-deck cargo space, or the galley may be located on the cargo level to provide more passenger space. Adjustable bulkheads permit loading both passengers and cargo on the main deck on some aircraft models. Some aircraft can be converted from passenger to freighter configuration in a few hours. None of these exceptions, however, lessens the usefulness of the joint production model in explaining the economics of air cargo, because the passenger-cargo proportions are not adjustable within the day-night cycle. An airline may optimize the proportions across its fleet and over time on a seasonal basis, but within the time frame relevant for analysis the assumption of fixed proportions is justified. See, for example, Civil Aeronautics Board Docket 22859 (Domestic Air Freight Rate Investigation), Opinion by the Board (August 18, 1977), p. 25.

nation aircraft. The determination of the costs of carrying cargo in these aircraft is a difficult analytical problem.[4] The efficient price for this service is determined by the joint supply function and the individual demand functions for passengers and cargo. This is the key to understanding the unusual regulatory history of the air cargo industry.

Cargo and passengers demand different scheduling and routing. Cargo seeks to move at night, with departures after 9 P.M. and arrival in the early morning hours; passengers prefer to travel in the morning and early evening. Cargo moves in one direction, from manufacturing centers to distribution centers; passengers make round trips to and from centers of commerce, production, and leisure activities. Cargo has no preference as to circuity, number of stops, or (generally) elapsed times under six hours; passengers strongly prefer nonstop flights. Cargo comes in many more sizes, shapes, and weights than passengers, and some shipments cannot physically or legally travel in combination aircraft.[5] Simply stated, combination aircraft cannot efficiently meet all the demands of both passengers and cargo. Were it not so, there would be no use for freighter aircraft—nor for all-cargo airlines.

Types of equipment employed and levels of demand are two elements in the economics of running an airline, and the scale and scope of operations is another. The few analyses of the air cargo industry raise the possibility that returns increase as firm size grows.[6] Given the much smaller size of cargo

4. See George W. Douglas and James C. Miller III, *Economic Regulation of Domestic Air Transport: Theory and Policy* (Brookings Institution, 1974), pp. 66–67, 76–79, 100–03; and James C. Miller III, "The Optimal Pricing of Freight in Combination Aircraft," *Journal of Transport Economics and Policy*, vol. 7 (September 1973), pp. 258–68.

5. Restricted articles include oversize shipments (too large to fit in a belly compartment), some live animals, and some hazardous (radioactive or toxic) materials.

6. Peter S. Smith, *Air Freight: Operations, Marketing and Economics* (London: Faber and Faber, 1974), p. 330; and Lewis M. Schneider, *The Future of the U.S. Domestic Air Freight Industry: An Analysis of Management Strategies* (Harvard Business School, Division of Research, 1973), pp. 94–106. Schneider, using pooled time series and cross section data, found no significant economies of scale for freighter operations, but conceded methodological flaws and noted the changing technology of the industry over the period of his study (1965–69). Studies of airline cost functions in general conclude that returns to scale are roughly constant over the range of firm sizes represented by the trunk passenger carriers. See Douglas and Miller, *Economic Regulation*, pp. 13–17; George Eads, Marc Nerlove, and William Raduchel, "A Long-Run Cost Function for the Local Service Airline Industry: An Experiment in Non-Linear Estimation," *Review of Economics and Statistics*, vol. 51 (August 1969), pp. 258–70; Mahlon R. Straszheim, *The International Airline Industry* (Brookings Institution, 1969), chap. 5, and app. B; and CAB Docket 33136 (North Central Airlines, Inc., and Southern Airways, Inc.), Bureau of Pricing and Domestic Aviation, Direct Exhibits, Testimony of J. Woodbury (October 1978).

operations relative to passengers, there may also be economies of scale in increasing traffic density.[7]

Fuller utilization of plant and equipment would realize what Panzar and Willig term economies of scope.[8] A large air carrier offering domestic and international service, scheduled and charter, over a large route network, may be analogized to a multiproduct firm with joint and common products. It may be able to produce each of its products at lower cost than if it were to specialize in a single product. Similarly, an airline's equipment can be used for its alternative mission during periods of slack demand for its primary mission. Or it can accommodate both passengers and cargo on a single aircraft. Because a large firm is more likely to be able to widen its scope, these economies are dependent on scale of operations. Potentially the greatest economy of scope would result from the integration of domestic and international cargo services. Time-of-day requirements are typically nonrivalrous, permitting increased use of aircraft and ground facilities without congestion; the coordination of flight connections and freight handling saves transactions costs. Thus a carrier that can secure international operating authority can raise the profitability of its domestic freight operation.

Theoretically, excess belly capacity would exist on most daylight domestic flights even if priced at incremental cost, but the extremely low passenger demand for late-night flights limits carriers' use of combination aircraft during this prime time for cargo. On international routes cargo constitutes a higher proportion of the total traffic, so combination aircraft do not offer sufficient cargo capacity. Freighters are the marginal source of supply during overnight hours on domestic routes and on the critical legs of international routes.[9] (More formally, because passenger and cargo space are available only in fixed proportions, the indicated supply price for cargo in combination aircraft exceeds the cost of providing the marginal supply in freighter aircraft.)[10]

7. See Theodore E. Keeler, "Domestic Trunk Airline Regulation: An Economic Evaluation," in vol. 6, *Study on Federal Regulation*, Hearings before the Senate Committee on Governmental Affairs, 96 Cong. 1 sess. (Government Printing Office, 1978), app., pp. 107–10.

8. John C. Panzar and Robert D. Willig, "Economies of Scale in Multi-Output Production," *Quarterly Journal of Economics*, vol. 91 (August 1977), pp. 481–93; and Robert D. Willig, "Multiproduct Technology and Market Structure," *American Economic Review*, vol. 69 (May 1979, *Papers and Proceedings*), p. 346.

9. Critical legs are those segments of an itinerary with the highest load factors and which are thus the capacity constraints for the entire trip.

10. A graphic exposition of these relationships is given in the appendix. A more formal

When demand for cargo capacity is low relative to passenger demand—as, for instance, on most daylight domestic flights—cargo will not fill the available capacity even when the allocation of aircraft cost is zero (price is set equal to incremental cost).[11] Of course, the price would never rationally be set below incremental cost over the long run. Thus one would expect to observe no price response to variations in cargo demand when the level of that demand is very low and price is set to incremental cost. At higher levels of demand, some aircraft (capacity) costs may be allocated to cargo, the proportion depending on the relative quantities of passengers and cargo. Under conditions of joint supply, higher levels of demand for one output increase the allocation of costs to that product—in effect, a rising cost situation. The elasticity of supply in combination aircraft is thus very low.

Freighters, however, effectively put a ceiling on the share of combination aircraft costs that can be allocated to cargo. When the price for carrying cargo in combination aircraft exceeds the price in freighters, the latter will enter the market and determine market quantity and price. Under these circumstances, the combination aircraft operator sets cargo capacity price at the freighter price and assigns remaining costs to passengers. Compared with the equilibrium in the absence of freighters, market price is lower for cargo and higher for passengers, cargo capacity and traffic are higher, and combination (passenger and cargo) capacity is lower.

These pricing models apply to an unregulated market. Regulation, in particular entry restrictions on air cargo and price controls for passenger service, however, generated inefficiencies and income redistributions.

Regulation

The Civil Aeronautics Board controlled the air cargo industry directly by setting rate levels and rate structures for cargo services and by assigning routes. Indirectly, by regulating prices for and entry into passenger air transportation, the board determined the capacity costs of providing cargo service in the belly of combination aircraft. Passenger fares for long-haul services, although lower on a per-mile basis, yielded relatively higher profits than did short-haul services. The frequency of service was increased on

development of models of unregulated air freight markets is given in Andrew S. Carron, "Deregulation of the Air Cargo Industry" (Ph.D. dissertation, Yale University, 1980).

11. Incremental cost, as used here, includes traffic servicing costs and the additional fuel necessary to transport the cargo, but excludes all other costs of aircraft operation and ownership.

long-haul (primarily transcontinental) routes, reducing passenger load factors and thereby narrowing the price-cost margin. Transcontinental service happened to correspond to the major domestic cargo traffic flows. As cargo and passengers are joint products in combination aircraft, the quantity of belly cargo capacity was correspondingly increased. The CAB did not control prices or entry for passenger or cargo service provided exclusively by small aircraft, a factor which was to become important by the time of deregulation.

In general, the board's practice was to permit cost-based rate changes upon application and to set maximum rates according to average total freighter costs (including a return on investment). Minimum rates were established at average noncapacity costs. Within this framework a highly variegated rate structure developed. The pricing flexibility afforded by discounts and premiums was intended to permit carriers to match rates to costs over a range of services, although the freedom to increase rates on prime-time service in selected markets was severely constrained. With declining costs of production, the board's infrequent examinations of maximum rates were unlikely to have much effect. Only in the late 1960s and in the 1970s did the rate ceiling become an issue.

The CAB regulated prices for cargo and passengers by rate averaging,[12] arriving at a nationwide standard based solely on shipment size and distance. The rates could be discounted for promotion of service or raised for hazardous or fragile goods. Given entry controls, standard rates meant that cost differences across markets would translate into differences among carriers in profits or service. Efficient aircraft and high load factors or utilization rates led to more profits. Yet the rate restrictions also prevented carriers from providing adequate service in certain high-cost markets (those with little or no backhaul, for example).

Regulation of entry was as stringent as control of rates. Statutory language required a new applicant to bear the burden of proof in demonstrating that the service would meet the test of "public convenience and necessity."[13] In practice, this meant that incumbent carriers could block entry on their routes. Essentially, the all-cargo carriers were confined to the routes they received when first certificated, in the late 1940s and early 1950s (to prevent them from competing directly with passenger carriers). And the

12. See Paul W. MacAvoy, *The Regulated Industries and the Economy* (Norton, 1979), p. 40; and Andrew S. Carron and Paul W. MacAvoy, *The Decline of Service in the Regulated Industries* (American Enterprise Institute for Public Policy Research, 1981), pp. 23, 28, 58.

13. Federal Aviation Act of 1958, Section 401 (49 U.S.C. 1371).

limited expansion of passenger-cargo authority permitted to passenger carriers increased prime-time cargo capacity very little.

The Industry under Regulation

Regulation of prices and entry in air cargo transportation resulted in specialization by the carriers according to the factors of production they were permitted to use. Only the passenger carriers could operate combination aircraft, generating cargo capacity as a joint product. Freighter aircraft could be employed in scheduled service by both passenger and all-cargo carriers. Small aircraft operations were unregulated, and so could be entered by any party. The use of trucks was restricted for all air carriers, forcing them to transport by air some shipments which could more economically move by surface for at least part of their trip.

Because of their equipment limitations, the commuter carriers could compete against larger equipment only over short-haul routes; in addition, the commuter carriers engaged in feeder operations and in the small parcel express business. All-cargo and supplemental (nonscheduled) carriers attempted to circumvent entry regulations by the regular chartering of aircraft to large shippers or leasing to other (usually overseas) carriers; no explicit route authority was required for these operations. This compartmentalization of functions was a product of regulation; an unregulated market would not have seen such specialization around factors of production.

Early Growth

The industry appears to have been well served—or, at least, not seriously hindered—by the first two decades of regulation. Air cargo grew at a spectacular rate during the 1950s and 1960s. Real output increased by 9 percent a year during the 1950s and by more than 17 percent a year during the 1960s.[14] Income growth and the development of domestic and international trade in high-value manufactured goods contributed to industry expansion. Changes on the supply side were more rapid and more profound than those on the demand side, and probably are the more important in explaining industry growth. Throughout this period, the air cargo industry was pro-

14. However, it had dropped significantly in the 1970s. See table 3.

Table 1. *Profitability in the Air Cargo Industry under Regulation, Certificated Route Air Carriers, Selected Years, 1963–77*

Percent

Type of service and carrier	*1963*	*1969*	*1973*	*1977*
	Operating margin, scheduled freighter operations[a]			
All services, all carriers	–25.0	2.0	1.1	6.1
Domestic service, all carriers	–33.1	–10.7	–2.1	4.7
Passenger carriers	–34.9	–7.7	–4.2	6.2
All-cargo carriers	–28.0	–26.0	5.0	1.5
International service, all carriers	–12.1	18.9	4.7	7.5
	Return on investment, all operations[b]			
All services, all carriers[c]	7.1	1.5	2.8	6.9
Passenger carriers[c]	7.5	1.6	2.7	6.7
All-cargo carriers	–2.3	–1.5	12.9	13.1

Sources: Author's calculations based on Civil Aeronautics Board, *Trends in All-Cargo Service* (CAB, 1977), pp. 2, 5; CAB, "Operating Results from Schedule All-Cargo Operations for the 12 Months Ended December 31, 1977," table 2; CAB, *Handbook of Airline Statistics* (GPO, 1969), pp. 201–13, 373–85; and subsequent issues; and CAB, *Supplement to the Handbook of Airline Statistics: Calendar Years 1973 and 1974* (GPO, 1975), pp. 46–82; and subsequent issues.

a. Net operating income divided by operating expenses.

b. Pretax return on property and equipment, adjusted for nonairline transactions.

c. Includes passenger operations of the passenger carriers.

vided with successive waves of more capacious and more efficient aircraft, rapidly expanding capacity while lowering real costs.

Paradoxically, the carriers reported that their domestic scheduled freighter operations were consistently unprofitable during the 1960s[15] (see table 1). The expansion in service offerings during this period suggests otherwise. Airlines reported high profits on their international and nonscheduled operations, and received substantially higher prices than the depreciated book values when they sold their used aircraft. Such factors indicate that costs, particularly aircraft capital costs, may have been overstated and that too many of the costs (or too few of the revenues) were allocated to domestic scheduled service.

Constraints on Growth

Regulation was incapable of adjusting to the changes of the early 1970s: geographic shifts in demand, increases in the price of jet fuel, and changes in the air cargo services of passenger and commuter air carriers. Demand for commercial airlift to Southeast Asia decreased as the level of military

15. Lucile Sheppard Keyes, *Regulatory Reform in Air Cargo Transportation* (American Enterprise Institute for Public Policy Research, 1980), pp. 12–14.

involvement there declined. In the United States the industrial areas of the North and Midwest, where air cargo service was concentrated, were losing population and industry to the South and Southwest. Thus demand for charter services fell as rapidly after 1969 as it had risen in the preceding years, and growth of the scheduled industry slowed to one-fourth its previous rate.

The fuel price increases after 1974 hit the air cargo industry particularly hard. All-cargo carriers had pretax profits of $35.9 million in 1973 but earned only $7.5 million the following year on the same volume of traffic; passenger carriers increased their profits from $325.6 million to $532.3 million during the same period, also without an increase in traffic.[16] Costs were also beginning to rise in nominal terms. Inflation was rising. And efficiency improvements of the jets were no longer contributing to increased profits. These rising costs would soon collide with regulatory constraints, forcing the carriers to increase rates or curtail service.

Also during the early 1970s passenger carriers began to use wide-body aircraft, whose cargo capacity ratio to passenger capacity was greater than old combination aircraft. The passenger carriers no longer added to their freighter fleets. All-cargo carriers also ceased adding new aircraft. Although their share of scheduled traffic increased in 1970, it remained constant thereafter until deregulation. In 1977, the year before the deregulation period began, domestic cargo revenues from scheduled certificated air service were $1.3 billion.[17] Intercity motor freight carriers, the closest substitute for air freight, had revenues of $31.0 billion.[18]

The unregulated commuter air carriers rapidly expanded their cargo operations during the 1970s. Their traffic increased at an average annual rate of 17 percent between fiscal 1970 and fiscal 1978.[19] Even so, the unreg-

16. Net income before income taxes, system operations. CAB, *Supplement to the Handbook of Airline Statistics: Calendar Years 1973 and 1974* (GPO, 1975), pp. 7, 46, 48–49. Data for the passenger carriers include passenger operations, as cargo expenses are not reported separately.

17. By comparison, scheduled domestic airline passenger revenues were $13.5 billion. CAB, *Supplement to the Handbook of Airline Statistics: Calendar Years 1977 and 1978* (GPO, 1979), p. 42.

18. Bureau of the Census, *Statistical Abstract of the United States, 1979* (GPO, 1979), pp. 634, 636. Only $7.5 billion were from small shipments, under truckload size, whereas nearly all of the air cargo shipments fell into this category.

19. Cargo tons enplaned. CAB, "Commuter Air Carrier Traffic Statistics: 12 Months Ended June 30, 1978" (CAB, 1978), p. 3. Mail is included in the calculation although distinguished from cargo by the CAB in this publication.

ulated carriers transported less than 5 percent of total domestic air cargo at the time of deregulation.[20]

At the time, this segment of the industry did not see itself as competing directly with the certificated carriers. Generally serving smaller markets and shorter routes, the commuter industry provided feeder service complementary to the larger carriers. One firm, Federal Express Corporation, aggressively promoted a new service, overnight door-to-door nationwide transportation of very small packages, that was well suited to the small aircraft permitted by the commuter air carrier exemption. Several of the commuter carriers, including Federal, had grown large enough by the mid-1970s to require some larger aircraft, which they could not operate without certification. These commuter carriers were unwilling to engage in the protracted, costly, and uncertain administrative process of certification—and were unable to secure congressional dispensation. Thus regulation constrained their ability to grow.

Distortion of Service

Passenger airlines and the board agreed that combination aircraft were scheduled for the benefit of passengers. Surplus revenue from cargo service was to subsidize passenger service. Revenue-offset costing reflected this philosophy: cargo rates used industry average freighter costs, and an estimate was made of the revenues forthcoming at those rates from cargo carried in combination aircraft. The passenger fare structure was then reduced by a percentage corresponding to the average contribution of freight revenues. As long as there was excess belly capacity, according to this reasoning, diversion of traffic to all-cargo carriers meant higher passenger fares.

The CAB thus disregarded the appropriate role of freighter aircraft and of all-cargo carriers. While it is true that efficiency required that cargo be carried in the bellies of combination aircraft to the extent possible, the board failed to appreciate the inferiority of combination aircraft in providing prime-time cargo service. The all-cargo carriers, which could have carried much of the overnight freight, were denied access, resulting in inefficiency in many prime cargo markets. Absent price controls, prime-time cargo rates would have increased above the freighter supply price, and capacity would have held to a level below that which freighters would

20. Ibid.; and Federal Aviation Administration/Civil Aeronautics Board, *Airport Activity Statistics: 1977* (FAA/CAB, 1978).

Table 2. *Price and Cost Changes in Domestic Air Cargo Service, 1956–77*

Period	Average annual percentage changes	
	Costs[a]	*Prices*[b]
1956–61	n.a.	0.5
1961–69	−5.7[c]	−2.1
1969–73	−0.7	3.0
1973–77	8.6	9.4

Sources: Author's calculations based on CAB, *Trends in All-Cargo Service* (CAB, 1977), p. 16; CAB, "Operating Results from Schedule All-Cargo Operations for the 12 Months Ended December 31, 1977," table 2; CAB, *Handbook of Airline Statistics* (GPO, 1961); and subsequent issues; and CAB, *Supplement to the Handbook of Airline Statistics: Calendar Years 1973 and 1974* (GPO, 1975); and subsequent issues.

n.a. Not available.

a. Expenses per cargo revenue ton-mile in freighter service.

b. Revenues per cargo revenue ton-mile in all services.

c. Calculation based on partial data.

provide. Given price controls, excess demand was manifested in higher cargo loads for the prime-time passenger flights and hence a reduction in the quality of service.

Although there is no clear pattern of refusal to grant cost-justified rate increases (see table 2), there is evidence that maximum rate regulation prevented some service expansion in the early 1970s.[21] Rates, however, given nationwide rate averaging, were not sensitive to cost differences across markets, times of the day, and commodities. Carriers began selectively reducing service in unprofitable markets. (A graphic exposition of this and other constrained markets is in the appendix.)

The profit-maximizing strategy of the passenger carriers was then clear: cargo was to be priced at or below the freighter costs of the all-cargo carriers; most traffic would travel in bellies at high rates of return; and some freighter service would be provided at a loss by the passenger carriers to retain the business of large air freight forwarders, the majority of whose traffic would move in bellies. For the all-cargo carriers, the appropriate reaction was also apparent: petition the CAB to set rates sufficiently high to cover average freighter costs (even if it meant more profits for the passenger carriers), and operate the most efficient freighter aircraft to make a profit when rates are at industry average costs.

Since cargo rates were determined according to industry average costs,

21. See CAB Docket 22859, Opinion of the Board, pp. 42–46. In his initial decision, the administrative law judge in the investigation recommended an increase of 38.8 percent in the average level of air freight rates, but by then the carriers had curtailed or eliminated many of their losing services. Ibid., p. 2.

carriers with below-average costs could achieve a combination of better service, more discounts, or a higher rate of return. Where high-cost and low-cost carriers competed, the low-cost carriers determined the price-quantity-quality level for all. (In the major East-West traffic lanes across the northern part of the country the passenger carriers, and then Flying Tiger Line, established the norms.) The availability of belly capacity also acted as a constraint on excess returns to low-cost freighter operators. Markets served by only high-cost carriers—those, for instance, in the South and Southwest that some cargo carriers sought unsuccessfully to enter—would have lower quality service and normal profits. Entry control provided protection for inefficient technologies in this manner.

Ultimately, freighter flights were eliminated from many markets. Shippers increasingly had to delay shipments until daylight hours, when belly space was available. Elapsed time for door-to-door transportation was double prime-time transportation, but prices were usually the same. Although some traffic was diverted to truck, and growth in demand was reduced by the higher (real, quality-adjusted) rates, the inelasticity of demand for prime-time service assured increased revenues while capacity (aircraft) costs to passenger airlines were reduced by the elimination or reduction of freighters.

Prime-time traffic which was diverted to surface or off-peak air movement due to these effects of regulation on capacity amounted to between 3 and 7 percent of all domestic air freight.[22] The lack of suitable airlift reduced total domestic scheduled freight traffic to a level by 1977 approximately 13.6 percent below what it would have been in the absence of regulation.[23] Where competition from all-cargo carriers did exist, the passenger carriers reduced but did not eliminate their freighter offerings. The reductions in freighter departures during the early and mid-1970s were concentrated in those markets where passenger carriers were sheltered from competition with all-cargo carriers. And in these markets, cargo traffic growth was flat or increasing coincident with the sharp declines in freighter service.[24]

An uneven distribution of international certificates and the attempt by the International Air Transport Association cartel to maintain high international cargo rates allowed certain carriers to engage in price discrimination. Carriers with both domestic and extensive international routes re-

22. Author's calculation.

23. Ibid.

24. See tables 4 and 5.

served space on their domestic freighter flights for international customers, who could be charged the higher international rates. Domestic shippers and international shippers who used another carrier for the international portion of the trip were charged lower rates but had less assurance of getting their shipments on the desired flight. U.S.-flag carriers with only international routes could offer the higher-priced service but were not permitted to fill up their aircraft over domestic segments with purely domestic cargo.

Inefficiency in Production

Rate and entry control caused carriers to operate their equipment inefficiently and discouraged the adoption of more efficient technologies as they became available. For example, Flying Tiger's aircraft carried capacity loads eastbound from the Orient to the United States. Westbound traffic over the Pacific was substantially less, but oil production on the North Slope would have used Tiger's capacity between the lower forty-eight states and Anchorage had not entry regulation prevented Tiger from carrying any of this traffic on its backhaul (every flight stopped in Anchorage for refueling). So Tiger's planes were flying partly empty over the same traffic lanes and at the same times as aircraft added by the carriers with traffic rights and those chartered by shippers. Seaboard World Airlines and Pan American World Airways were similarly handicapped on their flights between the interior of the United States and gateway airports. These production losses are estimated at $3.7 million in 1977—roughly 3.5 percent of these three carriers' domestic scheduled revenues.[25] Efficiency losses from preventing Federal Express to use larger, more efficient aircraft were $12.1 million in 1977, nearly 20 percent of estimated aircraft operating costs for the carrier and 9.4 percent of its estimated freight revenues.[26] These estimates do not include losses attributable to reduced traffic growth resulting from the higher rates charged to offset the costs of production inefficiency.

Further, the Interstate Commerce Commission (ICC) prohibited airlines from transporting cargo by truck except within twenty-five miles of the airports they were certificated to serve, and then only in conjunction

25. Author's calculations based on data supplied by CAB Docket 33712 (Tiger International-Seaboard World Airlines Acquisition Proceeding), Response to Order 79-2-131 of Tiger International (March 29, 1979), pp. 22–65; and CAB, *Supplement to the Handbook of Airline Statistics: Calendar Years 1977 and 1978*, pp. 54, 64.

26. Author's calculations based on Federal Express Corporation, *1978 Annual Report*, p. 13; and Federal Express, "First Quarter Report, August 31, 1978."

with air movement. These regulations forced air carriers either to serve many cities directly by air, increasing the costs of producing a given quality of service, or to contract with a regulated motor freight carrier for pickup and delivery, reducing the service quality at a given cost. Coordination between truck and air schedules is less reliable when there are two firms involved. Although shippers were willing to pay for trucking services that were more rapid and more dependable than standard less-than-truckload service, ICC regulations did not allow higher rates for faster service.

Production efficiencies which might have grown from product diversification are difficult to ascertain. Demand for scheduled air cargo transportation is seasonal and varies geographically. Demand for charters is also cyclical. Passenger carriers could reconfigure and redeploy aircraft within the limits of their route certificates, as traffic demand shifted, but the only options for the all-cargo and supplemental carriers during periods of low demand were to charter or lease aircraft to carriers with less restrictive route certificates. (This implies redistributions of income.) In practice, the aircraft lease market has been very fluid; under some leasing arrangements the operational control of an aircraft has changed on a weekly, daily, or even hourly basis. But even if leasing and chartering of equipment and facilities prevented any losses in production (and one ignored problems of asymmetrical bargaining), these arrangements nevertheless involved important transactions costs.

Regulated firms consider record-keeping, administrative process, and delay costly and inefficient. The air cargo industry's singular lack of success in winning concessions from the regulatory agency explains the reluctance of potential entrants to apply for new operating authority. Perhaps the most important transactions cost of regulation is the delay between changing market conditions and approval for new services or rates—during which the carrier operates less efficiently than it would in the absence of regulation. Inherent in regulatory proceedings is the cost of uncertainty: the carrier must plan for both favorable and unfavorable outcomes; it will be disinclined to take risks.

Conclusion

Stated in qualitative terms, the costs of regulation may be seen in the reduced efficiency of the industry and in the redistributions of income. It is possible to advance the analysis, to produce estimates of the misallocations in physical units—tons of cargo denied prime-time service, aircraft-miles used inefficiently—as has been done for some of the effects noted. A precise estimate of the dollar costs of regulation, however, requires an exercise in econometrics which lies outside the scope of this paper. Specifically, it would be necessary to know the elasticity of demand with respect to changes in service quality—what price would shippers denied prime-time space have been willing to pay for the assurance of accommodation, in addition to the charges for the daylight space actually used. Further, some estimate would be required of the potential demand discouraged or diverted to other modes by the lack of space. So, while it may be said with some certainty that the costs of air cargo regulation were substantial, precise quantification must await further research.[27]

It is possible, however, to provide a crude estimate of the efficiency losses. Applying conservative assumptions regarding the elasticities of demand with respect to price, income, and service quality, gross revenues were depressed by $165.7 million, allocation losses in 1977 were $41.5 million, and production losses (incurred by the international cargo carriers and by Federal Express) were $15.9 million—a total efficiency loss due to air freight regulation of $57.3 million in 1977, the last year before decontrol, or 5.1 percent of the industry's gross revenues that year.[28]

By the mid-1970s, the distortions caused by airline regulation had become acute. The growth of the economy had slowed with the recessions of 1970 and 1974, affecting especially the procyclical air cargo industry. The increase in fuel costs sparked high economywide rates of inflation. The regulated air cargo industry had difficulty changing service to match changes in shippers' demands. The response of industry and government to the emerging conditions was to consider regulatory reform.

The Deregulation Debate

Initially, the carriers attempted to bring about change through the CAB administrative process. Under the increasingly reform-minded guidance of chairmen John E. Robson and Alfred E. Kahn, the board itself undertook a series of actions aimed at reducing controls. The Domestic Air Freight Rate Investigation (DAFRI) begun in 1970 was still open. A number of

27. The data requirements to make the necessary calculations are discussed in Carron, "Deregulation," pp. 123–26.

28. Dollar losses are author's calculations; percentage based on CAB, *Supplement to the Handbook of Airline Statistics: Calendar Years 1977 and 1978*, p. 42.

carriers had applications pending for extensions of route authority. Most of these routes would have permitted the applicants either to fill gaps in an existing route structure or to extend service to the growing cities of the South and Southwest. Some of the commuter carriers were seeking exemptions so they could operate larger aircraft over some routes.

But the administrative processes were overtaken by outside events. In June 1976, the CAB added its airline regulatory reform proposals to those previously introduced in Congress. Unlike measures offered by Senator Edward Kennedy and by the Ford administration, the board's legislation treated cargo independently of passenger operations, and called for more radical reforms. A similar measure was introduced at the beginning of the Ninety-fifth Congress in 1977. During this period of debate on legislative deregulation, the anticipated administrative reforms were not forthcoming. Flying Tiger did not receive its requested route extensions nor Federal Express its exemption to operate large aircraft, and the CAB was to delay its final decision in DAFRI until more than two years after the issuance of the administrative law judge's initial decision. Industry observers have speculated that these conservative actions by an otherwise progressive board may have resulted from a political decision not to take any administrative actions which would relieve the pressure on Congress for legislative reform. By the time Senate hearings were held in March 1977 the cargo carriers had joined together in their call for legislative reforms.

The passenger carriers participated actively in the legislative reform proceedings, but their testimony focused entirely on passenger transportation. Their lack of attention to cargo deregulation may be attributed to a perception that resources were best spent on concerted efforts to influence the pace and direction of change in passenger regulation. Had they spoken out, all except Pan American might have opposed the liberalization of all-cargo entry. (Pan Am had no domestic authority under regulation.) The domestic passenger carriers had been successful in increasing belly loads by withdrawing their own freighters from protected markets and so would not gain from this change. And the pricing rigidities of regulation affected the all-cargo operator more severely than the passenger carrier.

Some shippers testified in opposition to deregulation. For forwarders, deregulation meant new competition with the direct air carriers for door-to-door delivery of shipments. Direct shippers feared that pricing freedom would deprive them of recourse in the event carriers chose to restrict service and raise prices. But under questioning, none of these witnesses could challenge the ability of an unregulated market to promote efficiency and improved service.

In the final stages the legislative process moved quickly. Although hearings on the comprehensive (passenger and cargo) reform bill continued until October 19, 1977, discussions between the House and Senate sponsors were already under way to separate the cargo sections from the more controversial passenger legislation.[29] Lawyers for Flying Tiger and Federal Express worked actively with the committees to guide and speed the process.

On October 20, 1977, Senator Howard Cannon proposed an unprinted amendment to a House amendment to a Senate amendment to the House bill (H.R. 6010) "to amend Title XIII of the Federal Aviation Act of 1958 . . . and for other purposes."[30] Among the "other purposes," as listed by Senator Cannon in his remarks to the Senate, was the following: "Eighth, the amendment would deregulate the all-cargo air transportation mode."[31] The amendment was approved on a voice vote. The bill soon returned from conference with a few changes and was agreed to by the Senate on October 28 and by the House on November 2. President Jimmy Carter signed the act into law on November 9.

Entry

Before amendment, the Federal Aviation Act required demonstration of public convenience and necessity before it granted a certificate to operate over a particular route. As a practical matter, this provision virtually precluded new entry on routes served by other carriers, regardless of the frequency or quality of the service provided. In the cargo deregulation debate,

29. The problems of cargo regulation were framed in terms of the service available to shippers and of the viability of the all-cargo carriers. Moreover, proponents of decontrol claimed the industry was sufficiently adaptive and competitive to risk a major regulatory change. See, for example, the statement of Joseph J. Healy, executive vice president and chief operating officer, Flying Tiger Line, in *Regulatory Reform in Air Transportation*, Hearings before the Subcommittee on Aviation of the Senate Committee on Commerce, Science, and Transportation, 95 Cong. 1 sess. (GPO, 1977), pp. 497–505. The debate on reform, however, never did demonstrate that Congress or the CAB understood the role of freighter aircraft in the air cargo market. The all-cargo carriers were seen as peripheral and thus of minor importance. But in fact these few firms (as the marginal sources of supply) would be the determinants of price and quantity in an unregulated market. And the important synergies between domestic and international service were largely ignored.

30. *Congressional Record, Daily Digest*, October 20, 1977, p. 34661.

31. Ibid., p. 34663. More precisely, the amendment deregulated prices for all domestic air cargo transportation and permitted free entry for the transportation of cargo carried in freighter aircraft.

some parties (such as the charter carriers) had urged retention of the provision in some form. Federal Express initially said that grants of entry on a regional basis would be sufficient,[32] and Flying Tiger similarly requested that entry "be permitted where the Board finds that an improved service would be provided."[33] These concerns were not differences of opinion on the ideal air cargo market but a struggle for preferential (or at least nondiscriminatory) treatment during the transition to free entry.

The early (1975–76) proposals, sponsored by Senator Kennedy and by the Ford administration, provided for a gradual relaxation of entry controls on the cargo industry as accompaniment to similar provisions for the passenger industry; under the administration bill, entry would never be completely open. The CAB's proposal, however, called for entry to be subject only to tests of the fitness, willingness, and ability of the applicant to provide the proposed service, without geographic restriction, shifting the burden of proof from the applicant to the opponent. It was essentially this language that was later embodied in the deregulation act.

The original proposal applied to "interstate all-cargo air transportation,"[34] which would have included cargo operations of the intrastate Alaska and Hawaii carriers and excluded Puerto Rico, the Virgin Islands, Guam, Samoa, and the Pacific Trust Territories. At the urging of Senators from Alaska and Hawaii, cargo operations within those states were exempt from the deregulation legislation. This exemption did not affect the long-haul interstate air cargo markets, the main targets of deregulation. Congress was persuaded to deregulate service to Puerto Rico and the Virgin Islands by Flying Tiger, which had sought to enter this lucrative market, then dominated by Eastern Air Lines, American Airlines, and Airlift International. (At one time, Flying Tiger had considered mergering with Airlift to acquire its operating rights in the South and Puerto Rico.)

Pricing

Another subject of debate was pricing flexibility. At one extreme were the shippers, who feared higher prices would cause them hardship, and carriers, such as Flying Tiger, which were concerned that abandonment of

32. Statement of Frederick W. Smith, chairman of the board, Federal Express, in *Aviation Economics*, Hearings before the Subcommittee on Investigations and Review and Subcommittee on Aviation of the House Committee on Public Works and Transportation, 94 Cong. 2 sess. (GPO, 1976), pp. 396–400.

33. Statement of Wayne M. Hoffman, chairman of the board, Flying Tiger, in ibid., p. 458.

34. S. 292, section 6(n). *Congressional Record, Daily Digest*, January 18, 1977, p. 1477.

minimum rates would lead to a destructive rate war and service cutbacks like those in the late 1940s. (In 1975 the administrative law judge in DAFRI had recommended retaining both minimum and maximum rates.) Even in its earliest proposals, however, the CAB had urged that price regulation be limited to the prevention of predation and discrimination and to the publishing of tariffs. As with entry controls, the pricing issue was resolved in favor of the least constraining alternative. Rates were to be considered legal unless found to be "unjustly discriminatory, or unduly preferential, or unduly prejudicial, or predatory."[35]

Transition

The CAB proposed granting nationwide operating rights immediately to holders of all-cargo certificates, with new entrants to be permitted these rights after two years. Carriers exempt from certification, such as Federal Express, thus would have been precluded from using larger aircraft during the transition period. While the board had in most other respects followed the recommendations of the special staff on regulatory reform, it did not accept the staff's plan in this area, which called for a two-year freeze on certificate holders while permitting new entrants immediately in those markets not receiving adequate service.[36]

These two positions represent divergent views as to the dynamics of adaptation to deregulation. The board had apparently accepted the arguments of the incumbent carriers, that they were burdened with plant and equipment mandated by thirty years of regulation and that they would be at a disadvantage compared with new entrants. The possibility that deregulation would render the existing capital stock suboptimal was one of the transition issues suggested above. Consider the following statement by Wayne M. Hoffman of Flying Tiger:

> I am sitting here with $200 million worth of stretch DC-8's which may not fit a completely unregulated type of market. . . . I cannot get from where I am now with equipment that may under that type of environment be obsolete or obsolescent to where I want to be simply overnight. In that period of time, a vested carrier is going to take a beating.[37]

35. Section 1002(d)(3) of the Federal Aviation Act of 1958, as amended (49 U.S.C. 1482).

36. Keyes, *Regulatory Reform*, pp. 24–25. Keyes was one of the five members on the special staff. She notes that "the CAB itself did not supervise preparation of the report and had no knowledge of its content before it was made public" (p. 25, n. 9).

37. *Aviation Economics*, Hearings, p. 474.

In effect, incumbent carriers feared that deregulation would force a decline in the market value of their assets. They were asking Congress and the administration to preserve their property rights. Regulation as practiced in its later years may or may not have created rents for the freighter operators —in a few instances, monopoly route certificates may have supported the continued operation of inefficient aircraft, creating a more robust resale market than might otherwise have existed. This issue is one of redistribution of income among incumbent carriers and between carriers and shippers. On the other side were the members of the special staff. They apparently felt that incumbency conferred advantages and that losses associated with existing plant and equipment were exaggerated.

Later versions of the deregulation bill followed the board's approach to the transition period but provided ever more sweeping coverage. By early 1977, the proposed legislation granted grandfather authority to both certificated and commuter (exempt) all-cargo carriers. In its August 1977 incarnation, grandfather rights were extended to passenger and supplemental carriers that used freighters and the transition period was shortened from two years to one. It was essentially in this form that the bill was enacted, except that the act required freighter service to have been continuous to qualify for unlimited domestic authority under the grandfather provisions. This change had the effect of excluding—allegedly inadvertently[38]—the supplemental carriers. A subsequent report on legislation to amend this oversight, however, contains this language:

> Delaying for 1 year the ability of supplementals to receive scheduled all-cargo authority would have an adverse economic impact on these carriers, yet to make them eligible immediately would adversely affect several scheduled cargo carriers who have been unable under their new authority to obtain larger aircraft, comparable to the aircraft operated by the supplementals. The committee selected the April 1, 1978 effective date so as to allow the scheduled cargo carriers time to obtain this equipment needed to place them on an equal footing with the supplemental carriers.[39]

The repeated changes in the legislators' position on this issue suggests that it was, in fact, an issue of income redistribution ultimately decided by the relative political weights of the all-cargo carriers and the supplemental carriers.

38. See Keyes, *Regulatory Reform*, p. 36, and her reference to statements made by the legislation's sponsors.

39. *Amending Title IV of the Federal Aviation Act of 1958*, S. Rept. 95-638, 95 Cong. 2 sess. (GPO, 1978), p. 2.

The Industry under Deregulation

In summary, the deregulation legislation contained the following provisions: that market forces would hereafter be the principal determinant of industry structure and performance; that existing operators of scheduled freighter service could apply for unrestricted domestic all-cargo authority beginning November 9, 1977, with certificates to be granted within sixty days; that existing operators of charter freighter service could apply beginning April 1, 1978, with certificates to be granted within forty-five days; that open entry for "any citizen of the United States" would begin as soon after November 9, 1978, as the board ruled on an applicant's fitness, willingness, and ability, but "no later than one hundred and eighty days after any application is submitted"; that Puerto Rico and the Virgin Islands would be covered; and that domestic cargo rate regulation for all carriers would be eliminated immediately except with respect to discriminatory or predatory pricing. The conference report stated the intention of Congress that rate tariffs continue to be published and followed, even though it was no longer required that they be filed with the CAB.[40]

Adaptation

Firms reacted to decontrol according to how much regulation was binding upon them—those most constrained reacted the sharpest. In general, the changes in the first years under deregulation were directed at improving production efficiency, increasing capacity and output, and enhancing prime-time freight services. Carriers entered new markets gradually, branching out from established service areas rather than jumping into wholly new regions. Price levels changed only modestly at first, and even with the sharper increases of 1979 and 1980, the adjustments were orderly and rational.

Income redistributions, however, were rapid. Revised asset valuations attributable to the expansion of operating authority were quickly capitalized. The common stock of the four publicly traded cargo airlines went up 25 to 50 percent in the two months immediately following deregulation and continued over the next two years (see table 3). Meanwhile, the Dow Jones transportation index (which had lost 2.2 percent during the year before

40. *Conference Report on H.R. 6010*, H. Rept. 95-773, 95 Cong. 1 sess. (GPO, 1977), pp. 14–15.

Table 3. *Share Values of Cargo Airline Stocks, Selected Dates, 1976–79*

Airline	*Dollars per share at end of month*			
	October 1976	*October 1977*	*December 1977*	*December 1979*
Airlift International[a]	0.11	0.19	0.25	0.69
Federal Express Corporation	2.03[b]	9.16[b]	34.75[c]	93.25[d]
Seaboard World Airlines	3.50	3.38	4.88	10.75
Tiger International	11.75	11.13	16.38	19.00
Memo:				
Dow-Jones transportation index	210.37	205.78	217.18	252.39
New York Stock Exchange index	54.89	50.65	52.50	61.95

Sources: Airlift International, direct communication (1980); Federal Express Corporation, *Annual Report,* selected years and *New York Times,* various issues.

a. Bid prices.

b. Per-share book value at end of preceding (May 31) fiscal year.

c. Closing price at end of first week of public listing (April 1978).

d. Price of $46.625 adjusted for 2:1 stock split.

cargo deregulation) increased only 5.5 percent during those same months and rose only 16.2 percent in the following two years. The performance of the New York Stock Exchange index was similar to that of the Dow Jones stocks. By 1980 the adjustment of share values to deregulation was complete, as the price change by that time reflected conditions peculiar to each firm rather than a general pattern.

Given the extensive investments made by carriers in the first years of deregulation and the unsettled condition of the national economy, conclusions on the ultimate profitability of the air cargo industry are speculative at best. Rates of return were down in 1978 as some carriers incurred start-up costs and others wrote off their inefficient aircraft.[41] As a result of an even weaker economy and even greater fuel prices, return on investment was negative in 1979 and 1980 (see table 4). The previously certificated scheduled carriers as a group reported an operating loss of $22.3 million for their domestic freighter operations in 1980. Some of the smaller all-cargo

41. Return on invested capital fell from 13.1 percent in 1977 to 6.2 percent in 1978 for the all-cargo carriers; pretax net income fell slightly as the value of property and equipment increased by one-half. Net income is adjusted to exclude nonoperating income. Author's calculations based on CAB, *Air Carrier Financial Statistics: December 1978* (GPO, 1979), pp. 2, 51.

Table 4. *Profitability in the Air Cargo Industry, Certificated Route Air Carriers, 1977–80*

Percent

Type of service and carrier	*1977*	*1978*	*1979*	*1980*
	Operating margin, scheduled freighter operations[a]			
Domestic service, all carriers	4.7	n.a.	4.4	−2.7[b]
Passenger carriers	6.2	n.a.	3.0	−4.8
All-cargo carriers	1.5	10.3	6.1	−0.3[b]
	Return on investment, all operations[c]			
All services, all carriers[d]	6.9	7.5	−1.1	−4.8[e]
Passenger carriers[d]	6.7	7.6	−1.0	−4.8[e]
All-cargo carriers	13.1	6.2	−3.9	−4.8[e]

Sources: Author's calculations based on CAB, "Operating Results from Schedule All-Cargo Operations for the 12 Months Ended December 31, 1977," table 2; CAB, *Supplement to the Handbook of Airline Statistics: Calendar Years 1977 and 1978* (GPO, 1979), pp. 41, 45, 77; CAB, "Summary of Section 418 Domestic All-Cargo Financial and Traffic Results for the Six Months Ended June 30, 1979," table 1; and subsequent issues, as revised; and CAB *Air Carrier Financial Statistics: December 1979,* pp. 1–2, 65; and subsequent issues.

n.a. Not available.

a. Net operating income divided by operating expenses.

b. Data for Airlift International excluded (not reported).

c. Pretax return on property and equipment, adjusted for nonairline transactions.

d. Includes passenger operations of the passenger carriers.

e. Year ended September 1980. Data for Seaboard World Airlines excluded (not reported).

carriers, however, such as Federal Express, continued to earn substantial profits during this period.[42]

Equipment and facilities that were efficient under regulation were even more so under deregulation. The older, fuel-intensive freighters, typically used for peak-hour service on noncompetitive routes, became unprofitable. There was a redistribution of income among carriers according to the efficiency of the aircraft owned at the time of deregulation. However, the prior distribution was based on regulatory artifice and not on the functioning of the market.

Shifts in service affected employment: new jobs, higher rates of pay for some; loss of employment and seniority, and the expense of relocation for others. The increased hiring associated with expansion, particularly by

42. CAB, "Summary of Section 418 Domestic All-Cargo Financial and Traffic Results," preliminary unpublished data (CAB, April 1981). The data on previously certificated carriers include freighter operations of passenger carriers but exclude Airlift International, which had not reported its 1980 results. Among the previously certificated carriers, Braniff International Airways, Northwest Orient Airlines, and United Airlines had small operating profits, but American Airlines, Pan American World Airways, Flying Tiger Line (including Seaboard World Airlines), and Hawaiian Airlines lost money. Federal Express reported profits of $88.1 million on revenues of $511.2 million.

Flying Tiger and Federal Express, is more easily isolated than adjustments to contraction. Labor provisions designed to ease the impact of cyclical fluctuations on airline employees, together with the growth in passenger service, have tended to mask any dislocations from cargo deregulation.

Constraints on Adaptation

Constraining influences still affected the growth of the air cargo industry after deregulation. Some of these were the inevitable slow adjustments to a changed market and disappeared as supply began to match demand. Others were economic regulations outside the influence of market forces.

The aircraft best suited to domestic air cargo are those with a low design density, large capacity, medium range, and moderate fuel consumption per unit of capacity. The small number of efficient used aircraft (mostly McDonnell Douglas DC-8-61s and Boeing 747s) available initially were quickly acquired by a few operators. At the time of deregulation, there was an order backlog of up to four years for new freighters to put into cargo service and new passenger aircraft to replace obsolescent passenger aircraft suitable for conversion to freighters.

The intermodal nature of air cargo transportation led to a concentration of freight traffic at a small number of hub and terminal points. Four airports (Chicago's O'Hare, New York's Kennedy, Los Angeles's International, and San Francisco's International) carry over 40 percent of all domestic air freight, although they carry less than 20 percent of the passenger traffic.[43] Space at two of these airports (O'Hare and San Francisco International) was at first so restricted that a carrier could expand only if another carrier relinquished some of its facilities.

Over the years CAB policy forced carriers to specialize geographically —those granted international authority were limited in their domestic routes. With deregulation, the international carriers (Pan American, Seaboard, Flying Tiger) faced no legal or administrative obstacles in expanding their U.S. operations, but the carriers with primarily domestic routes (American Airlines, Delta Air Lines, Eastern Air Lines, United Airlines) could not begin international service without securing approval of all the governments involved. International carriers have expanded domestically more than noninternational carriers, indicating the effects of international route authority on cargo operations under domestic deregulation.

43. Passengers and freight tons enplaned, 1978. CAB, *Supplement to the Handbook of Airline Statistics: Calendar Years 1977 and 1978*, pp. 140–41.

To the extent that the CAB continues to determine passenger fares, the imputed cost of cargo service will be affected. If maximum passenger rates are binding on the carriers, freight capacity in combination aircraft will be partially displaced by larger passenger loads, and the indicated cost of freight service will increase. This effect can be expected to disappear as the CAB reduces its control over passenger service and air carriers begin to depart from the standard industry fare level guidelines.

Environmental regulations promulgated by the Federal Aviation Administration and the Environmental Protection Agency require the older aircraft in domestic cargo service to be modified, reengined, or retired from service on a phased schedule beginning in 1981, with full compliance by the end of 1984.[44] The costs of these changes can be as much as $15 million for new engines on a DC-8-63.[45] It is not economical to modify or reengine the freighter Boeing 707s or the older DC-8s, and these aircraft will have to be scrapped or sold to foreign operators at low prices. The development of the domestic air cargo industry over the next few years will depend on how these regulations affect particular carriers. Carriers with relatively old (noncomplying) aircraft may be severely restricted in their ability to expand.

Service

During the first year of deregulation domestic traffic rose 5.7 percent for the certificated carriers and 28.9 percent for the noncertificated air carriers.[46] In the five years before deregulation the domestic certificated industry grew 1.8 percent a year and noncertificated carriers, 9.2 percent (see table 5). During 1979, air cargo output slowed following the massive cost increases brought about by fuel prices, with the economy itself expanding at a slower rate. Growth for the previously certificated carriers was almost flat that year; the noncertificated carriers continued their rapid increases.[47]

44. Federal Aviation Regulation 36, "Noise Standards: Aircraft Type and Airworthiness Certification" (14 C.F.R. pt. 36), p. 551.

45. Bruce Hagar, "New Life for Old Jets in Engine Jobs," *New York Times*, April 19, 1981.

46. After deregulation traffic between Anchorage and the lower forty-eight states on Flying Tiger was reclassified from international to domestic service, even though a substantial portion continued to be merely in transit to or from Asia. In 1978 this traffic was over 213 million revenue ton-miles. Comparisons of 1977 with 1978 data exclude Anchorage traffic; comparisons of 1978 with later years includes Anchorage traffic. See Keyes, *Regulatory Reform*, p. 40, n. 1.

47. Data for 1979 are affected by strikes against United (fifty-seven days) and Flying

Table 5. *Output Growth in Domestic Scheduled Air Cargo Transportation, 1973–80.*
Percent

Type of carrier	*Market share*[a]	*Average annual change* 1973–77	1977–78	1978–79	1979–80
Certificated route[b]	95.3	1.8	5.7	0.1	−2.3
Passenger[b]	84.6	2.1	2.6	−2.8	−3.6
All-cargo[b]	10.7	−0.1	27.0	12.1	2.2
Noncertificated	4.7	9.2[c]	28.9[c]	36.8[c,d]	26.8[e]
Memo:					
Total economy[f]	. . .	2.2	4.6	3.5	−1.3

Sources: Author's calculations based on CAB, *Supplement to the Handbook of Airline Statistics: Calendar Years 1973 and 1974* (GPO, 1975); and subsequent issues; CAB, *Air Carrier Traffic Statistics: December 1979;* and subsequent issues; CAB, "Commuter Air Carrier Traffic Statistics" (CAB, 1978); and subsequent issues; CAB, *Airport Activity Statistics of the Certificated Route Air Carriers* (GPO, 1979); CAB, "Summary of Section 418 Domestic All-Cargo Financial and Traffic Results for the Six Months Ended June 30, 1979"; and subsequent issues; *Economic Report of the President, January 1981*, p. 279; and *Federal Reserve Bulletin*, vol. 67 (February 1981), p. A46.

a. Share of domestic cargo revenue tons enplaned, year ending June 30, 1978.
b. Domestic scheduled cargo revenue ton-miles. Data for 1973–78 exclude Flying Tiger Line Anchorage traffic; data for 1978–80 include Anchorage traffic. See note 46.
c. Commuter air carriers, domestic scheduled cargo tons enplaned.
d. Calculation based on partial data.
e. Section 418-only carriers, domestic scheduled cargo revenue ton-miles.
f. Final production, total U.S. economy.

The inflation and recession in 1980 contributed to reduced levels of output for the previously certificated industry, while the smaller carriers continued to grow.

The quality of service was enhanced along with increases in traffic. Freighter service was expanded geographically and more and larger aircraft were added to existing routes. The first service under deregulation was transporting domestic cargo in conjunction with international service. Flying Tiger, which had used Anchorage for a servicing facility before deregulation, now enplaned and deplaned local cargo there. Pan Am began transporting domestic cargo to fill up its freighters on segments between coastal gateways and interior U.S. points. Carriers next began tying new cities into their networks. Flying Tiger initiated service from Chicago to Dallas-Ft. Worth, Houston, Atlanta, and other cities. Airlift extended its East Coast network to Seattle and Portland. Seaboard began a transcontinental domestic flight to link the Midwest and the West Coast with its transatlantic service.

These new services were initiated in the first year of deregulation by

Tiger (seventeen days), and by the grounding of DC-10 aircraft (forty days). See CAB, *Air Carrier Traffic Statistics: December 1979* (GPO, 1980), p. 117.

incumbent carriers seeking to establish themselves in new markets before entry was permitted to others in the second year. Often these services required the use of leased aircraft and makeshift ground facilities. As a consequence, service to the new cities was less reliable than it had been to cities served by the old networks, and even these were affected as connections were missed and aircraft delayed throughout the route. Nevertheless, the new services attracted significant amounts of traffic.

Pan Am's domestic scheduled traffic was up 66.6 percent in 1978 and another 6.4 percent in 1979 as that carrier was able to accept local domestic cargo for the first time. The major gainer among the all-cargo carriers was Flying Tiger, with an increase of 36.9 percent the first year and 3.2 percent the next.[48] Seaboard did not initiate domestic service until late in 1978, so year-to-year comparisons are not meaningful. That carrier's domestic traffic for 1979 amounted to 2.0 percent of total scheduled domestic cargo.[49]

Commuter air carriers began enlarging their fleets when freed from the maximum size restrictions that previously bound them. Several carriers acquired used turboprop passenger aircraft and converted them to freighter service. Federal Express immediately began acquiring jet freighters, each seven times the size of its largest aircraft under regulation; in 1980, it purchased two DC-10 wide-body freighters and increased the number of its Boeing 727 and 737 aircraft. In two years its daily volume increased 150 percent.[50]

The supplemental carriers were slower to take advantage of the opportunities under deregulation. First, they were mandated to wait until April 1978—six months after the scheduled freighter operators—before applying for authority to operate scheduled freighter flights. But their expansion was delayed also by the need to set up ground facilities and sales networks. Evergreen International Airlines did begin serving coastal routes in the

48. Flying Tiger's traffic growth may be overstated for 1978 and understated for 1979 when measured in ton-miles. The new operations in the southern tier initially routed all traffic through the Chicago hub, substantially increasing the mileage traveled compared with more direct paths. In 1979, East-West links across the southern tier were established. See CAB Docket 33712, Bureau of Domestic Aviation, Brief to the Board (April 16, 1980), p. 45.

49. Calculated by summing reported 74,230,000 revenue ton-miles for March through December 1979 and one-half of the "approximately 25 million scheduled revenue ton-miles . . . for the period November [1978] to February [1979] reflected in international which should have been reported as domestic." CAB, *Air Carrier Traffic Statistics: December 1979*, pp. 86, 117.

50. Three months ended August 31, 1977, and November 30, 1979. Author's calculations based on Federal Express, "First Quarter Report, August 31, 1977"; and subsequent issues.

East and West with two converted turboprop aircraft; Zantop International Airlines, a contract carrier of automobile parts from Detroit to various assembly points, started a scheduled service on the return trips; and Transamerica Airlines (formerly Trans International Airlines) provided some new service. But most of these carriers continued to transport cargo primarily under charter, within a limited route network. The charter carriers reported no scheduled freighter traffic for 1979 and less than 24 million revenue ton-miles for 1980.[51] This represents less than 1 percent of the scheduled cargo traffic carried by domestic carriers.[52]

The passenger airlines, which had served many points exclusively before deregulation, curtailed cargo service in response to entry by others. They apparently chose to devote their managerial and financial resources to the emerging problems and opportunities under passenger deregulation. Two years after cargo deregulation, the domestic trunk carriers' share of the domestic air cargo market had dropped from 76 to 68 percent (excluding Pan Am). The share accounted for by the previously certificated all-cargo carriers (plus Pan Am) increased accordingly, from 20 to 28 percent, with the remaining domestic passenger carriers (local service, Alaska, Hawaii, and so on) transporting about 4 percent over the period.[53]

In 1980, a major air freight forwarder (Airborne Freight Co.) acquired a small all-cargo airline (Midwest Charter Express) and became the first forwarder to operate its own aircraft fleet.[54] Two other forwarders—Air Express International and Profit by Air—also began to use their own aircraft in conjunction with the scheduled lift of the direct air carriers. But examples of new firms or of firms in related industries entering the market are conspicuously few. No motor freight companies or railroads chose to become airlines. Most major air freight forwarders continued to use scheduled and chartered aircraft operated by direct air carriers rather than assume operational control themselves.[55]

Traffic growth was accommodated with relatively modest additions to

51. CAB, "Summary of Section 418 Domestic All-Cargo Financial and Traffic Results for the Six Months Ended June 30, 1979" (CAB, November 19, 1979); and subsequent issues, as revised.

52. Ibid., preliminary unpublished data (April 1981); and CAB, *Air Carrier Traffic Statistics: December 1980* (GPO, 1981).

53. CAB, *Air Carrier Traffic Statistics: January 1978* (GPO, 1978) and subsequent issues.

54. *Seattle Times*, May 7, 1980.

55. Emery Air Freight, the largest forwarder, acquired the authority to operate its own aircraft shortly after deregulation but later relinquished that right when it decided to continue using the established airlines (*Aviation Daily*, March 14, 1980).

Table 6. *Prime-Time Cargo Capacity in the 200 Largest City-Pair Markets, Fourth Quarters, 1977 and 1978.*

Market description	Number of city pairs		Prime-time load factor[a] (percent)	
	1977	*1978*	*1977*	*1978*
All markets	200	200	61.7	56.6
No freighter service[b]	68	63	61.9	56.9
Freighter service[b]	132	137	61.7	56.4
No all-cargo carriers[c]	116	109	63.7	57.7
All-cargo carriers[c]	84	91	59.1	55.3
Freighter service added in 1978[b]	...	17	66.2	53.5
All-cargo carriers added in 1978[c]	...	15	64.7	59.4

Sources: Author's calculations. Data on weight traffic and departures by aircraft type and carrier type by city pair supplied on computer tape by CAB, Economic Regulation 586 Segment Data (October, November, December, 1977 and 1978); conversion of traffic weight to volume based on average densities by type of traffic as reported in CAB Docket 22859 (Domestic Air Freight Rate Investigation), Opinion by the Board (August 18, 1977), p. 27; aircraft capacities from Special Reports provided pursuant to CAB Order 79-2-131; flight departure times from *Official Airline Guide* (October 1977 and 1978); and *Air Cargo Guide* (October 1977 and 1978); volume of passenger baggage calculated as product of thirty-five pounds per seat, number of seats, and stowed baggage densities as used in CAB Docket 22859 (DAFRI) and Docket 23080 (Priority and Non-Priority Mail Rates), Exhibit BE-IR-2701. Sample includes 200 largest (directional) city-pair markets (by 1977, fourth quarter, cargo volume transported) for domestic markets (including Alaska, Hawaii, and Puerto Rico) reporting scheduled nonstop flights performed in fourth quarters of both 1977 and 1978. Capacity and cargo are based on space, with cargo data converted from weight data. Load factor of 100 percent is assumed for city pairs with no prime-time service. Ratios are unweighted means of ratios across city pairs. Passenger baggage loads are assumed at 100 percent of passenger capacity.

a. Prime time applies to departures scheduled between 9:00 P.M. and 6:59 A.M., inclusive. The load factor is the ratio of cargo transported to capacity offered, and is used to indicate general availability of space for prime-time cargo; lower number implies better availability of space.

b. Includes freighter operations of both trunk and all-cargo carriers.

c. Applies to service provided by Airlift International, Flying Tiger Line, and Seaboard World Airlines, only.

capacity, which increased only 2.5 percent in 1978.[56] Domestic cargo capacity increased another 5.2 percent from 1978 to 1979, and rose 5.7 percent during 1980.[57] These aggregates, however, are unenlightening because they include large amounts of capacity affected by changes in the operations of combination aircraft which are not relevant for cargo traffic.

Table 6 indicates the extent to which the new service improved prime-time space availability. Whereas before deregulation the load factor was substantially higher in markets not served by all-cargo carriers than in markets with their service, after passage of the legislation there was almost no difference between the two markets. The lower the load factor, the better the availability of cargo space. Thus the threat of entry by an all-

56. Domestic available cargo ton-miles, scheduled service; Flying Tiger traffic to and from Anchorage is excluded (see note 46).

57. Flying Tiger traffic to and from Anchorage is included. Author's calculations based on CAB, *Air Carrier Traffic Statistics: December 1978* (GPO, 1979), p. 4; and subsequent issues.

cargo carrier improved prime-time service in all markets after deregulation. Most of the fifteen city-pair markets newly served by all-cargo carriers were points in the southern tier; rerouting of prior transcontinental service across the northern tier account for the rest.[58] For these markets, the improvement in space availability implies a diversion of traffic from combination aircraft to freighters and from surface transportation to air. In the first year of deregulation, service expanded sharply to areas previously closed to the all-cargo carriers. Cities that had lost freighter service, where passenger carriers had faced little or no competition from the all-cargo carriers, gained the most when deregulation opened those markets.

During the first year of deregulation, nationwide freighter departures, which had fallen consistently in the years before deregulation, increased 9.2 percent (see table 7). Cities with no all-cargo carriers, previously, gained the most freighter departures and cargo traffic. Even cities that had adequate freighter service registered gains, in sharp contrast to the years immediately before deregulation.

In 1979 the pattern shifted markedly. Freighter departures fell across all city types but were especially sharp in those that gained service in 1978. In part, the reduced numbers of departures represent only the substitution of nonstop for multistop service—the initial expansion had been limited by equipment shortages and start-up costs, and a single aircraft would collect cargo at multiple points. But more fundamentally, the service reduction was a winnowing of carriers themselves. The number of cities receiving freighter service continues to grow, but fewer airlines are available at each point.

In mid-1978 Trans World Airlines disposed of its entire fleet of inefficient Boeing 707 freighter aircraft and subsequently offered only belly capacity to its shippers. Its domestic cargo traffic fell 13.4 percent from 1977 to 1978 and another 12.2 percent the following year,[59] and air cargo service to points in the Midwest it alone had served, notably Indianapolis, Dayton, St. Louis, and Kansas City, was reduced. (Flying Tiger has since initiated freighter service to St. Louis and Kansas City.)

Seaboard's domestic transcontinental service, begun in the year follow-

58. Southern tier points are Atlanta, Charlotte (N.C.), Dallas-Ft. Worth, Houston, Miami, and San Juan. The northern tier encompasses the West Coast, the Midwest, and the Northeast.

59. Revenue ton-miles. CAB, *Air Carrier Traffic Statistics: December 1978*, p. 42; and subsequent issues. Pan Am also phased out its Boeing 707 freighter operations but increased overall capacity with its timely acquisition of Boeing 747 freighters.

Table 7. *Freighter Departures and Traffic, Domestic Flights, 1971–79*
Percent

Market description and output	Change over period[a]			
	1971[b]–73	*1973–77*	*1977–78*	*1978–79*
No all-cargo carriers[c]				
Freighter departures	−39.1	−68.7	+64.6	−35.4
Cargo tons enplaned[d]	+22.2	−0.8	+21.8	−7.8
Restricted all-cargo carriers[e]				
Freighter departures	+0.5	−42.2	+32.6	−9.4
Cargo tons enplaned[d]	+17.6	+13.6	+7.8	+1.8
Unrestricted all-cargo carriers[f]				
Freighter departures	−8.1	−29.7	+6.1	−14.9
Cargo tons enplaned[d]	+22.9	+0.1	+7.0	−3.0
Sample cities total				
Freighter departures	−11.9	−35.8	+12.7	−15.6
Cargo tons enplaned[d]	+21.9	+1.9	+10.0	−3.3
U.S. total				
Freighter departures	−14.0	−36.2	+9.2	−16.3
Cargo tons enplaned[d]	+20.7	+0.6	+9.1	−2.8

Memo:

Output	Sample cities' share of U.S. total				
	1971[b]	*1973*	*1977*	*1978*	*1979*
Freighter departures	92.7	94.9	95.5	98.6	99.3
Cargo tons enplaned[d]	84.8	85.7	86.8	87.5	87.0

Source: Author's calculations based on CAB, *Airport Activity Statistics of the Certificated Route Air Carriers* (GPO, 1971), and subsequent issues. Calculations reflect domestic departures of the certificated route air carriers, excluding intrastate operations of the Alaska and Hawaii carriers; sample cities are those representing 85 percent of fiscal 1971 cargo tons enplaned.

a. Not annualized.
b. Fiscal year ending June 30.
c. Cities not authorized to be served in domestic service by any certificated scheduled all-cargo carrier before deregulation.
d. Includes combination and freighter aircraft.
e. Cities authorized to be served only by Airlift International or Seaboard World Airlines before deregulation. See text.
f. Cities authorized to be served in domestic service by Flying Tiger Line before deregulation.

ing deregulation, was incorporated into Flying Tiger's service following the merger of those two carriers. Airlift has eliminated virtually all of its domestic service including the Seattle and Portland flights added after deregulation, but most of these routes still have at least one freighter operator.[60] Evergreen has also reduced service begun since deregulation. Domestic

60. In fact, Airlift's service reductions have followed closely Flying Tiger's entry into those markets. Flying Tiger has also applied for CAB approval to take over Airlift's international routes, which would mean the incorporation of all three previously certificated all-cargo carriers into a single firm. CAB Docket 38850 (Application of the Flying Tiger Line for an Exemption from Section 401), Order (January 14, 1981).

Table 8. *Price and Cost Changes in Domestic Air Cargo Service, 1973–80*

	Average annual percentage change		
		Prices	
Period	*Costs*[a]	*Average yield*[b]	*General commodity rates*
1973–77	8.6	9.4	10.9
1977–78	6.6	7.8	11.9
1978–79	12.8	11.8	13.7
1979–80	25.2	13.5[c]	n.a.

Sources: Author's calculations based on CAB, *Supplement to the Handbook of Airline Statistics: Calendar Years 1973 and 1974* (GPO, 1975); and subsequent issues; CAB, *Trends in All-Cargo Service* (CAB, 1977), p. 16; CAB, "Operating Results from Schedule All-Cargo Operations for the 12 Months Ended December 31, 1977," table 2; CAB, *Air Carrier Traffic Statistics: December 1979*, p. 4; and subsequent issues; CAB, *Air Carrier Financial Statistics: December 1979*, p. 2; and subsequent issues; CAB, Office of Economic Analysis, "For Information" Memorandum to the Board (March 5, 1980), app. C; CAB, "Summary of Section 418 Domestic All-Cargo Financial and Traffic Results for the Six Months Ended June 30, 1979," table 1; and subsequent issues; and CAB, *Aircraft Operating Cost and Performance Report*, vol. 12 (CAB, July 1978), pp. 3, 8; and subsequent issues.

n.a. Not available.

a. Expenses per cargo revenue ton-mile in freighter service.

b. Revenues per cargo revenue ton-mile in all services.

c. Calculation based on partial data.

freighter flights have been reduced by all of the passenger airlines which operate them.

Rates

Rates increased significantly during the first two years of deregulation, as indicated in table 8. Cost inflation slowed in 1978, as deregulation brought gains in productivity, but began rising again in 1979. This may be largely attributed to the doubling of domestic aircraft fuel prices during 1979,[61] as airline cargo profit margins did not show increases over the prederegulation period. Although these signals are ambiguous, they do suggest that average rates were not far out of line at the time of deregulation.

There was one general rate increase during 1978. Most carriers increased their prices by an average of 8 to 10 percent in March or April of that year; carriers that had adjusted rates late in 1977 waited until later in the year. The second round of increases, in January and February of 1979, was less uniform. Carriers that operated freighters added somewhat more than those using only combination aircraft. Further rate changes occurred

61. CAB, "Fuel Cost and Consumption: December 1979" (CAB, 1980); and subsequent issue.

over the second half of 1979. By the end of that year, rates for the major freighter operators (American, Flying Tiger, United) were almost 40 percent above those at the time of deregulation. Rates charged by airlines operating only combination aircraft (Continental Air Lines, Delta, Trans World) were up somewhat less, from 22 to 33 percent.[62] This pattern, however, is not unlike that observed before deregulation: the major freighter operators (American, Flying Tiger, Trans World, United) increased rates by twice as much on average as carriers operating no freighters (Continental, Delta).[63] Despite a softening of demand in 1980, costs forced further rate increases. In the first six months of 1980 cargo costs rose at an annual rate of approximately 39 percent.

The rate structure also changed, reducing the misallocations that previously existed. And with passenger deregulation, carriers can eliminate cross subsidies between passengers and cargo by adjusting the rates for each to reflect the economics of joint production in combination aircraft. With improved service, fewer shippers are paying premiums for guaranteed service, and with increased competition on some routes more discounts are being offered. Shipments tendered in containers and those of relatively high density are accorded lower per-pound rates in line with operating economies. Cargo tendered at off-peak times (days and weekends) is also carried at a discount because it fills what otherwise would be unutilized capacity. Rates on shipments requiring special handling—live animals, hazardous articles, human remains—are up sharply. Surcharges for these items had been insufficient under regulation, and carriers were reluctant to accept them.[64] As a result of the discount traffic, the average yield on freight shipments increased by less than the general commodity rates (see table 8).

Two issues related to rate policy arose following deregulation: liability for cargo and filing of rate schedules. Under regulation carriers were liable for loss of and damage to shipments up to $9.07 per pound.[65] Following deregulation, a number of carriers lowered their standard liability limits to 50 cents per pound. Shippers complained to the CAB and to Congress, but

62. Based on CAB, Bureau of Pricing and Domestic Aviation, "For Information" Memorandum to the Board (March 27, 1979), pp. 1–5; and CAB, Office of Economic Analysis, "For Information" Memorandum to the Board (March 5, 1980), app. C.

63. Ibid.

64. See Alfred E. Kahn, "Air Freight Forwarding in an Era of Regulatory Reform," speech delivered at Air Freight Forwarders Association, June 2, 1978.

65. CAB Docket 19923 (Air Freight Liabilities and Claim Rules and Practices Investigation), Order (March 22, 1976).

the prevailing view was that low liability limits were neither inefficient nor inequitable. And all carriers offered higher limits for a surcharge.

The CAB had also required, under regulation, that carriers file rate tariffs with the board. In response to deregulation, the CAB eliminated this requirement:

> We came to the conclusion that it was really not at all necessary to file tariffs in order to get information out to shippers about what the rates are, that the carriers would get that information out very efficiently without filing tariffs.
>
> We then looked at the question of discrimination and preferential, predatory, prejudicial pricing, keeping in mind that we did not retain the power to suspend tariffs once they were filed. . . . We thought that we could retain our freedom to take such action in the event of discrimination by requiring that the carriers retain records and way bills and all the information that would be necessary to establish discrimination. . . .
>
> On the negative side, we were concerned with the anticompetitive aspects of the filing of tariffs, because it tended, we thought, to result in uniform pricing.[66]

The board was concerned that the uniformity of pricing would discourage rate competition. Filing of official tariffs would be a means of tacit collusion and, because tariffs must be followed once filed, would restrict the ability of carriers to initiate or match price cuts. Shippers objected to elimination of the tariff filing requirement, apparently because they believed the carriers' own rate sheets would no longer be available: "While airline observers expected few changes as a result of the 'total deregulation' of the cargo industry Nov. 9 [1978], some concern was expressed that cargo prices could go 'wild' now that the CAB no longer requires filing of tariffs."[67] However, shippers have not encountered such problems. The issue remains contentious, however, as Congress clearly intended to preserve the tariff requirement.[68]

Transition

During the transition process, as firms adjusted to change, there were short-run shortages of production inputs, hoarding, rationing, and decisions based on misperceptions of the future. Carriers expanded so rapidly in attempts to preempt competitors that the reliability of service deteriorated.

66. Marvin S. Cohen, chairman of the CAB, in *Regulation of Air Cargo Freight Transportation*, Hearing before the Senate Committee on Commerce, Science, and Transportation, 96 Cong. 1 sess. (GPO, 1979), p. 62.

67. *Aviation Week and Space Technology*, November 6, 1978, p. 36.

68. Conference Report on H.R. 6010, pp. 14–15.

Many new discount rates were implemented, found to be either unremunerative to the carrier or unattractive to the shipper, and subsequently withdrawn. Shippers incurred additional costs in obtaining information about the wider array of prices and services available. The unregulated environment was perceived as qualitatively different by some, and firms engaged in extensive and costly contingency planning. Although it is too early to tell, investors may now demand increased rates of return to compensate for the perceived greater uncertainty of the unregulated environment, but this is presumably offset by greater opportunities for efficiency and expansion. Predictions of "transitional chaos," however, were not fulfilled.[69] Information on the actions of competitors, customers, and suppliers was freely available. The ability to adjust rates and services as carriers learned about the deregulated market was relatively unencumbered. Although some firms may eventually fail, it will not be because of losses incurred as a result of mistakes made in reaction to the transition environment.

Effect on Equilibrium

A more serious concern is the effect of the transition on the eventual equilibrium of the industry. The deregulation act permitted scheduled freighter operators to begin new service several months before their counterparts in the supplemental (charter) industry and more than a year ahead of everyone else. This timetable, which was the subject of much of the debate over the reform legislation, appears not to have constrained any carrier. Except for Flying Tiger and Federal Express—which, by virtue of their role in the reform process, may have anticipated the final legislation—no carrier was prepared to offer service before permitted to do so under the act. Though it may be argued that the nongrandfather carriers failed to act because of the transition rules, examination of technological problems in initiating service and of carriers' own statements suggests that they either would not or could not have acted differently.

However, the transition rules did enhance rather than counteract variations among carriers in their mobility, profitability, and opportunities for expansion. A few established carriers reaped short-run gains. These firms possessed several factors of production then in short supply—efficient aircraft, facilities at overcrowded airport cargo terminals, access to capital markets, managerial skill, and fuel at contract rates—on which they

69. Hoffman in *Aviation Economics*, Hearings, p. 474.

earned rents and by means of which they grew relative to their rivals. One manifestation of this was increasing concentration in the industry, even with much small-scale entry.

This pattern may be a cause for concern when viewed in conjunction with other changes. The reductions of service described above were not the result of rationalization but rather of large carriers growing and small ones declining. (The opposite pattern is taking place in passenger air service: small carriers are growing and concentration is decreasing.) Moreover, cargo load factors have increased despite the weaker economy. The competitiveness of cargo markets, which was intense immediately after deregulation, may now be in decline. The top four firms accounted for 62 percent of the scheduled domestic cargo traffic in 1980, up from 55 percent in January 1978.[70] Control over the marginal source of supply, freighter aircraft, has become even more concentrated. In 1977, the four largest operators carried 83 percent of the domestic traffic moving in freighters; by 1980, the share had risen to 94 percent.[71] Among the large carriers, Flying Tiger has grown while the remainder are static or in decline. Flying Tiger carried 22 percent of the total domestic cargo traffic in 1980, representing 54 percent of the freighter traffic.[72] A few of the former commuter carriers have also done well, although only the largest of these—Federal Express—ranks with the previously certificated carriers.[73]

Another indication of concentration are the mergers involving major cargo carriers that have operating authority on international routes. A market failure may have been established by the transition policy, which

70. Flying Tiger traffic to and from Anchorage is included (see note 46). The data do not include the operations of carriers such as Federal Express that are now large firms as a result of deregulation but that did not report their traffic on a consistent basis in 1978 and 1980. CAB, *Air Carrier Traffic Statistics: January 1978*; and subsequent issues.

71. CAB, "Operating Results from Schedule All-Cargo Operations for the 12 Months Ended December 31, 1977" (CAB, 1978); and CAB, "Summary of Section 418 Domestic All-Cargo Financial and Traffic Results," selected issues 1979–80. These data include only carriers with certificates during regulation, as the operations of carriers such as Federal Express were not reported on a consistent basis in 1977 and 1980. Including these carriers in the 1980 tabulation would lower the share of the four largest carriers from 94 percent to 85 percent. Federal Express, with a share of 8 percent, thereby replaces Northwest as the fourth largest freighter operator.

72. CAB, *Air Carrier Traffic Statistics: December 1980*; and CAB, "Summary of Section 418 Domestic All-Cargo Financial and Traffic Results," preliminary unpublished data (April 1981). Including the operations of the new carriers would give Flying Tiger a 47 percent share of the domestic scheduled freighter traffic.

73. Federal Express reported 166.9 million scheduled cargo revenue ton-miles for 1980; all other new carriers reported 98.0 million. Total domestic scheduled cargo traffic in all aircraft types was 4,483.4 million.

confers on the large incumbents what would otherwise have been only short-run advantages. The test of this hypothesis will come as carriers adjust to slow economic growth, the continuing pressure of higher operating costs, and a market structure characterized by an increasing size disparity between the large and small firms.

Policies

A few general rules for designing transition plans can be suggested, although they should be considered tentative at this point. The development of a more formal model, incorporating the determinants of the transition path identified here, will permit a more rigorous test of the hypotheses and the development of guidelines for the effective conduct of public policy toward regulated industries.

A brief period between the passage of legislation and its implementation and a short transition period would maximize efficiency and avoid major disruptions. An elaborate schedule for phased decontrol prolongs the distortions of regulation and introduces new opportunities for mistakes and reversals by the regulators. Immediate and complete changes provide some predictability about the regulatory environment.

Uniform treatment of new entrants and incumbents would avoid giving advantages to one group. The costs of having operated under regulation are largely sunk, while the strengths carry over into the new unregulated world. New entrants face the more formidable obstacles under deregulation.

Identification of possible deviations from desirable paths would assure that the anticipated equilibrium will be reached. Mergers, acquisitions of control over critical resources, and investment decisions can lead to a long-run equilibrium that is socially inefficient. But the corollary to this point is that continued or phased regulation should not be used as the means of addressing such problems. Rather, the generally applicable control mechanisms—antitrust, legislative oversight, judicial review—should be readied for possible use.

Information and rapid resolution of problems would foster smooth adjustment. When the air cargo industry was deregulated, the CAB suspended many data reporting requirements. The board's preoccupation with the passenger industry means there are only perfunctory reviews of the cargo industry's adjustment. Oversight by the Justice Department, the Department of Transportation, or the Federal Trade Commission will begin only at the end of the passenger deregulation transition period between

1983 and 1985. The gap in information and oversight responsibility can mean a bumpy transition.

Conclusion

Important lessons can be learned from the deregulation of the air cargo industry. First, redistributions of income occur quickly and seem relatively insensitive to transition policies. Two, efficiency losses during the adjustment period, while likely, seem not to be a cause for concern. The advantages of the new service offerings clearly outweigh short-run adjustment costs. Third, transition policy seems to have had its most important consequences in the establishment of long-run equilibrium. The path that was followed brought major structural changes. It has also influenced investment decisions, choice of technology, and long-run patterns of pricing and profitability in the industry.

Cargo deregulation was more than a simple repeal of the existing legislation. Policies for a phased implementation were debated at length. These discussions, however, were grounded in concerns over past harms. The transition decisions were weighed according to the private calculus of the firms rather than by standards for the economy as a whole. Transition was, in fact, a means of gaining support for reform and not a means of implementation. The likely path of adjustment was not explicitly analyzed. Important factors, such as the synergies among products and the joint production technology, were overlooked. Yet policy choices crucially affected the transition, generally increasing the flexibility of established scheduled carriers while restricting potential entrants. The advantage to existing carriers perhaps has determined the eventual structure of the industry.

Several other industries, formerly subject to rigid economic regulation, are now also in the process of adjustment. The airline passenger, rail, and motor freight industries are operating under phased deregulation. Similar rules have been applied in the decontrol of natural gas and petroleum prices, and in the provision of certain telephone products and services. Less closely related, substantial segments of the securities and consumer banking industries have been deregulated. Taken together, these sectors represent a large share of the national economy now in the process of adjustment.

A number of tentative findings can be advanced applicable to any deregulated industry. Firm and industry adaptation to deregulation is qualitatively different from adaptation to regulation. Uncertainty is increased rather than decreased, the means of ameliorating the effects of prior decisions (grandfathering) are less clear, and advance knowledge and action can confer advantages. The transition path resulting from regulatory change can be characterized by the interaction of basic economic objectives (such as profit maximization) with the institutional and technological constraints which are binding at each point during the adjustment process. Such constraints, and the differential rates at which they bind and relax, can impose inefficiencies and income redistributions.

Firms' reactions to these effects can generate further distortions. They will attempt to shape the transition process (the pattern of institutional constraint relaxation) to minimize the bottlenecks they are likely to encounter while maximizing the restrictions on competitors.

Policy decisions before deregulation shape the path of adjustment and the final equilibrium. Policy authorities, therefore, assuming their objectives are to maximize efficiency gains and to act impartially, must make two determinations in designing regulatory reforms. First, of course, they must compare the existing state with the equilibrium projected under the proposed regime. Then they must find a path leading to that new equilibrium. Static models of the unregulated industry are inadequate predictors of the course of adaptation and the ultimate results. A sequential model of industry adjustment is required, taking into account factor endowments, political influences, technical and resource constraints, the extent of initial disequilibrium, type of regulation, and alternative policy approaches to deregulation.

A number of factors may indicate potential problems in the deregulation of an industry. In the air cargo industry the existence under regulation of high market concentration or a dominant firm, capital intensity, economies of scale or scope, the continuation of some regulatory constraints, and the control of critical resources affected transition. Explicit treatment of these factors can facilitate and improve regulatory reform. Specifically, undesirable income distribution and resource allocation effects of transitions can be reduced with appropriate policies.

A clear perception of the goals of regulatory reform and a consensus on the legitimacy of property rights established and revoked through the regulatory process is the central requirement, however. With planning and analysis, the specter of disruptive transitions will be real only if the parties to the process—through inattention, poor planning, or lack of will—choose to make it so.

Appendix

The models of air cargo markets discussed in the text are presented here graphically. Alternative examples of an unregulated market are developed and used to examine distortions induced by economic regulation.

For analytical convenience, the costs of transportation are divided between capacity and noncapacity. Only the allocation of capacity costs is shown. The passenger or shipper may be thought of as purchasing capacity separately, and noncapacity costs are not joint between passengers and cargo. Thus no allocation problem exists for noncapacity costs.

Shapes of the curves are arbitrary, which does not affect the generality of the results. Capacity cost per aircraft mile is shown as *SS'*, where the *x*-axis (*Quantity*) represents tons of passenger and cargo capacity in fixed proportions for combination aircraft. The sum of demands for passenger plus cargo capacity is shown as *DD'*. The demand curve for cargo alone is shown as *dd'* (of course, demand for passengers alone could be constructed by subtracting *dd'* from *DD'*).

The case of low cargo demand relative to passenger demand (daylight flights, for example) is shown in figure 1. The static equilibrium for combi-

Figure 1. *Unconstrained Airline Market with Low Cargo Demand, Combination Aircraft Only*

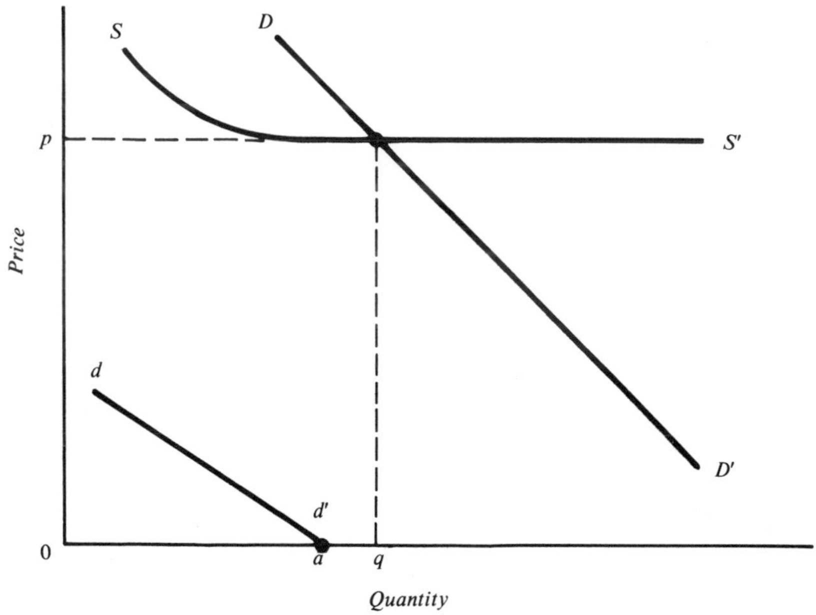

Figure 2. *Unconstrained Prime-Time Air Cargo Market, Combination Aircraft Only*

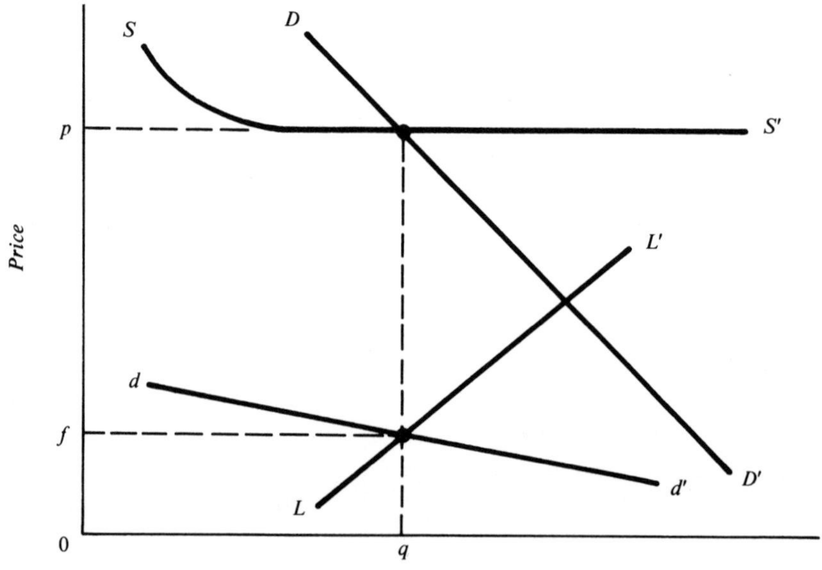

nation aircraft occurs at the intersection of *DD'* and *SS'*, with *q* tons of capacity provided at a price *p* above noncapacity costs. Only *a* units of cargo traffic will move paying only noncapacity costs, even though capacity is *q*. Passenger traffic will equal capacity *q* at a price *p* representing all of the capacity costs of the aircraft.

The more general case, shown in figure 2, allocates combination aircraft (capacity) costs between the two products, passengers and cargo. The equilibrium quantity of joint capacity is *q* at price *p*, with cargo paying *f* and passengers paying $(p - f)$. The set of equilibrium price-quantity relationships for cargo is *LL'*, which is the locus of points found by subtracting the difference between *DD'* and *dd'* from *SS'*.

As cargo demand increases, the use of freighter aircraft modifies the analysis, as shown in figure 3. In the absence of freighters, the diagram is analogous to figure 2, with equilibrium at price *p* and quantity *q*. Suppose, however, that freighter capacity is available according to the price schedule shown by curve *FF'*. (This curve necessarily lies below *SS'*, since for a given aircraft type, more cargo space is available at a given price when the aircraft is in freighter configuration; therefore, a given quantity is supplied at

Figure 3. *Unconstrained Prime-Time Air Cargo Market, Combination and Freighter Aircraft*

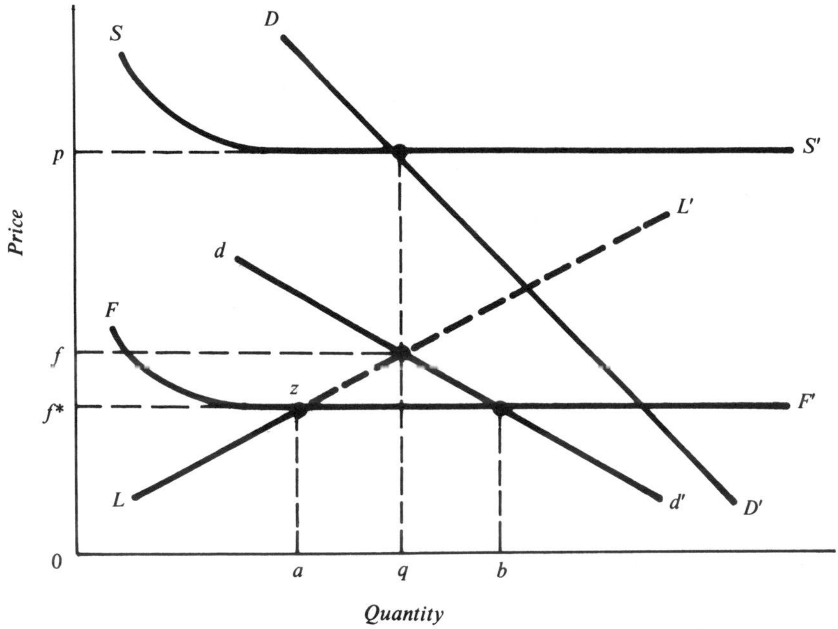

a lower price.) The equilibrium cargo price is reduced from f to f^*, and the passenger price increased from $(p - f)$ to $(p - f^*)$. At these new prices, the passenger market clears at quantity a, less than before. The cargo market now clears at b. Combination aircraft are only supplying a units of joint capacity; the remainder, $(b - a)$ units of cargo capacity, is supplied in freighter aircraft. The equilibrium price-quantity set for cargo when freighter service is available is LzF' rather than LzL'.

Regulation forced a deviation from these efficient results. Entry controls prevented the operation of freighters in some city-pair markets. The result might have been higher prices for cargo, as shown in figure 3: a cargo price of f clears the market at joint quantity q. But prices were controlled as well, nominally at the level of freighter costs (shown as f^*). Industry demand for cargo service at that price was more than the amount supplied. Figure 4 illustrates the case of excess demand: industry demand at the controlled price f^* is b, the quantity of joint capacity supplied is only a, and excess cargo demand is $(b - a)$. The unconstrained cargo demand curve is shown as $d''d'$. This excess demand was manifested in a reduced quality of service. In particular, the mean and variance of shipment time increased as load

Figure 4. *Air Cargo Market with Constraints on Rates or Freighter Entry.*

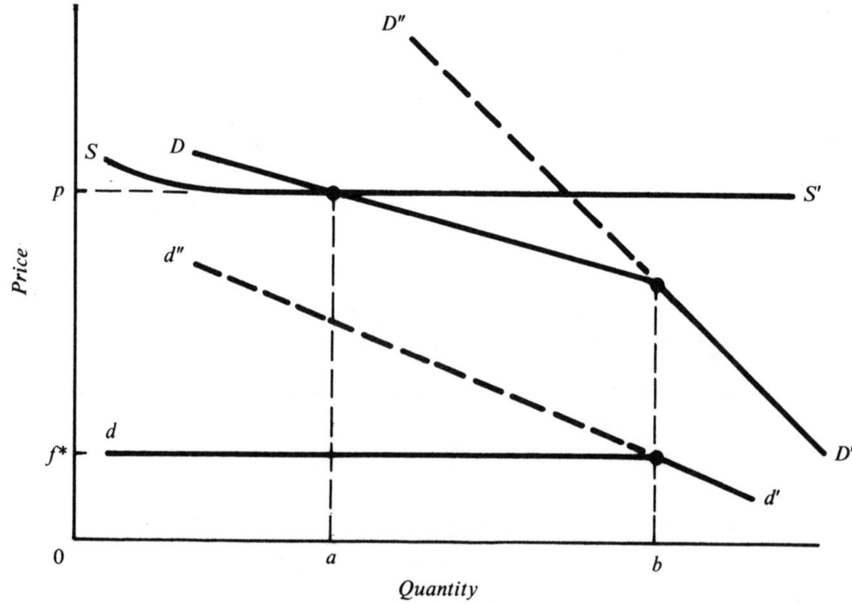

factors rose. Price ceilings set below the cost of freighter service had identical results. The determining factor was whether or not freighters were able to supplement combination aircraft.

The CAB also controlled passenger fares. Consider a market in which the price for passenger service is fixed by regulation at P_p, above the competitive level, but where cargo rates are not controlled. This case is shown in figure 5. The passenger demand curve is d_pd_p'; the unconstrained demand curve is the downward-sloping broken line *ee'* intersecting d_pd_p' at quantity *a*. Unconstrained market demand for passengers plus cargo is *EE'*. Combination capacity is supplied in a quantity *a* that clears the market for passenger service at the regulated passenger price. There is a discontinuity in the locus of market-clearing cargo rates *LL'*. In particular, any additional cargo capacity supplied by combination aircraft incurs the full aircraft capacity cost *C*, while the inframarginal units incur only a fraction of the capacity costs. At the price P_a which clears the market for cargo (given the quantity determined by passenger demand), there are excess profits made of amount $(P_p + P_a - C)a$.

Figure 5. *Air Cargo Market with Constraints on Passenger Fares*

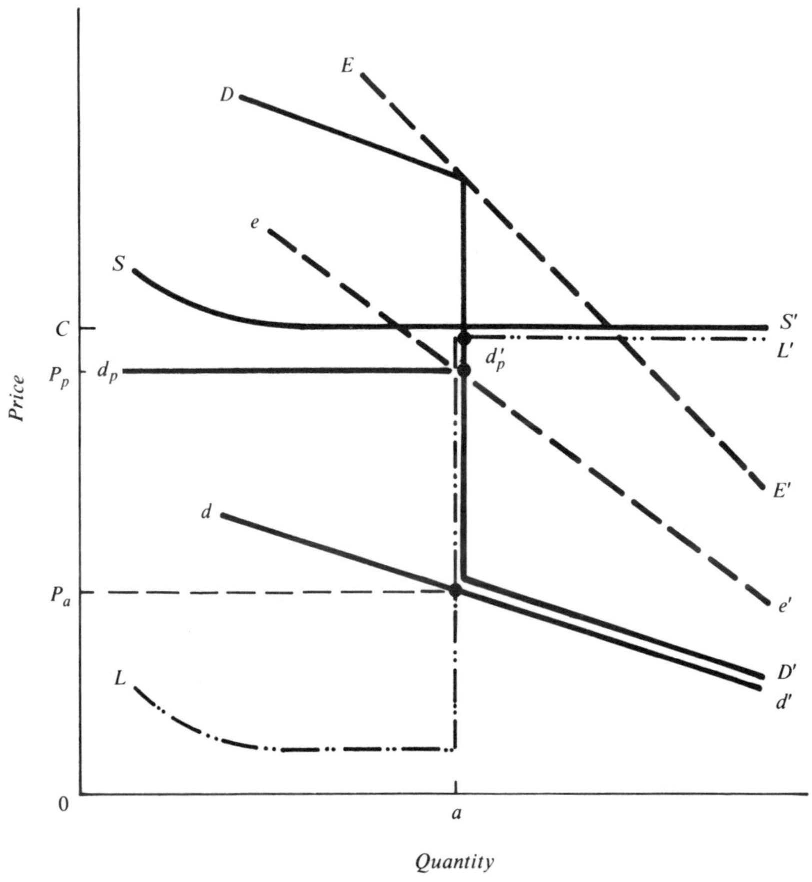